# Salt Journals

*Middle East Literature in Translation*
Michael Beard and Adnan Haydar, *Series Editors*

---

For a full list of titles in this series,
visit https://press.syr.edu/supressbook-series
/middle-east-literature-in-translation/.

# SALT JOURNALS

## Tunisian Women on Political Imprisonment

Edited by
**Haifa Zangana,**
**Christalla Yakinthou,**
and **Virginie Ladisch**

Translated from the Arabic by
**Katharine Halls** and **Nariman Youssef**

Syracuse University Press

∞ The paper used in this publication meets the minimum requirements
of the American National Standard for Information Sciences—Permanence
of Paper for Printed Library Materials, ANSI Z39.48-1992.

For a listing of books published and distributed by Syracuse University Press,
visit https://press.syr.edu.

ISBN: 9780815638513 (paperback)
9780815657279 (e-book)

**Library of Congress Cataloging-in-Publication Data**

Names: Zangana, Haifa, 1950– editor. | Ladisch, Virginie, editor. | Yakinthou, Christalla,
1980– editor. | Youssef, Nariman, translator. | Halls, Katharine, translator.
Title: Salt journals : Tunisian women on political imprisonment /
Haifa Zangana, Virginie Ladisch, and Christalla Yakinthou ;
translated from the Arabic by Katharine Halls and Nariman Youssef.
Description: First edition. | Syracuse, New York : Syracuse University Press, 2024. |
Series: Middle East literature in translation | Includes bibliographical references.
Identifiers: LCCN 2024027788 (print) | LCCN 2024027789 (ebook) |
ISBN 9780815638513 (paperback) | ISBN 9780815657279 (ebook)
Subjects: LCSH: Arabic essays—Tunisia—Translations into English. |
Arabic essays—Women authors—Translations into English. | LCGFT: Essays.
Classification: LCC PJ8256.5.E5 S25 2024  (print) | LCC PJ8256.5.E5 (ebook) |
DDC 892.7/46089287—dc23/eng/20240921
LC record available at https://lccn.loc.gov/2024027788
LC ebook record available at https://lccn.loc.gov/2024027789

*Manufactured in the United States of America*

Those who read the past incorrectly will also read the present and future incorrectly; we must know what happened in the past so as to avoid repeating the same mistakes. It would be foolish to pay the price of our mistakes twice over.

—Abdelrahman Munif (1933–2004)

# Contents

# Foreword

## Creative Writing: The Unseen Fabric of Prison

### Haifa Zangana

I happened to be in Tunisia when I was approached by Bahithat, the Lebanese Association of Women Researchers, and asked to contribute to their seventeenth annual publication, titled *Time: Testimonies and Paths of Inquiry*. During the period of political liberalization that followed the revolution of January 14, 2011, when many political prisoners were released, Tunisia's literary scene saw the publication of a number of prison memoirs. I'd also recently finished editing *Party for Thaera: Palestinian Women Writing Life*,[1] a collection of works by liberated Palestinian *asirat*[2] about their time in the jails of the Israeli occupation.

Given the circumstances, it was only natural for me to choose to write about something that linked all these things together. My article was titled

1. The idea of organizing creative-writing workshops for former women political prisoners was born during my visit to Toronto in 2004. I was invited by Iranian academic and activist Shahrzad Mojab, a professor at the University of Toronto, to give a lecture, "How and Why: Reassessing Memory and Building the Future." The idea developed further when Professor Mojab invited me again in 2007 to colead the workshop "Imperialist Feminism and Women's Memoirs." This workshop included a number of Iranian leftist activists who had been imprisoned in Iran during the eighties. The women participants were encouraged to tell their stories—and consistently working with Mojab, they did. I undertook the same project in Palestine. The workshops, which I led in Ramallah over a period of two years, have resulted in *A Party for Thaera*.

2. Captive political Palestinian women in Israeli jails often released in prisoner exchanges or political deals.

"Preliminary Observations on Prison Time: The Writing of Tunisian Political Prisoners."

I wanted to include writings by female political prisoners, but as I collected and surveyed the books that had been published, I found to my surprise that not one woman had written about her prison experience.

I wasn't only surprised because I knew hundreds of women of varying political allegiances had been detained during the presidencies of the late Habib Bourguiba and the ousted Zine El Abidine Ben Ali. Women political prisoners haven't, in general, been heard enough in the Arab world. What was surprising about the case of Tunisian women prisoners was the general impression, shared across the region and globally, that Tunisian women enjoy political and cultural advancement far beyond their sisters in other Arab countries. Tunisian women played prominent roles in the anticolonial struggle and were decisive in building the postindependence state. Where, then, were the voices of Tunisian women writing about experiences that must be existentially significant—and also significantly different from those of other women, such as Palestinians? Or had they chosen to "speak silence," to borrow a phrase from Argentinian poet Alejandra Pizarnik?[3] There are plenty of reasons that women political prisoners, and Arab women more generally, might "speak silence" and shun writing and publishing. So I was told by Palestinian Asirat during a creative-writing workshop I led in Ramallah, Palestine, in 2016. Their message was repeated by Tunisian women political prisoners, despite their very different circumstances, during a creative-writing workshop organized by the International Center for Transitional Justice and the University of Birmingham, in the United Kingdom, in 2017–18, as part of a project titled "Voices of Memory."

An introductory session was held on September 20, 2017, and attended by nine Tunisian women who were participating in the "Voices of Memory" project. Many questions were raised. What was a creative-writing workshop, and what was its aim? How is creative writing different from other artistic and literary forms that can be used to record and document

3. Alejandra Pizarnik (born April 16 or 29, 1936, Buenos Aires; died September 25, 1972), poet whose poems are known for their stifling sense of exile and rootlessness.

experiences? Isn't it enough for others to record or write down female prisoners' testimonies on their behalf? Is it actually possible to convey an experience to the reader "better," or with more "style," by learning the techniques of literary writing? Or are writers born with an innate talent, making writing workshops a novelty but ultimately a waste of time and money? We also spent some time on a critical examination of books by male former political prisoners that had been published in Tunisia since the revolution.

### A Creative-Writing Workshop?

The idea was simple: women should write their own stories instead of having others write for them. The writing would be different from the texts being widely produced for the purposes of documentation (though that task is hugely important in itself). The stories would be creative, retaining the details and human depth so often neglected by the writers of history as tangential or unworthy of recording. All the participants had their own, exceptional, stories, and all they needed was to develop the literary techniques necessary to commit them to paper. Their stories would be their own, but they would be woven into the fabric of a wider struggle.

We also talked about selecting other participants to join those women already present at the workshop and agreed on two basic conditions. First, the workshop would be open to any woman who was either a former political prisoner herself or the relative of one and had shared the hardships that prisoners had faced for opposing the dictatorship or exercising their freedom of opinion. Second, participants had to want to write. Priority would be given to women who had previously tried their hand at writing, of whatever kind—letters, vignettes, journals, short stories, poetry, and so on.

The first session of the workshop, held on January 29, 2018, was attended by nineteen women from all over the country, of different professions (including a lawyer, an engineer, a nurse, a student, a company director, a city council member, a university student, a teacher, and civil society activists), aged from their twenties to their late sixties. What they all had in common was the prison experience of the eighties and nineties. Seventeen went on to attend the following three workshops (held in Sousse, Dar Zaghouan, and Hammamet), and the texts they produced ultimately became this book—an idea that developed gradually, but soon became a goal that the participants worked toward eagerly and ambitiously.

### Why Doesn't She Write?

In the first workshop, the question came up again: Why don't we write? It occupied most of our attention. After discussing it in detail, we realized it was actually multiple questions. Why might Arab and Tunisian women choose not to write? Why might women write less than men? Why do women political prisoners in particular not write about their experiences, while their male counterparts produce book after book? This idea raised an equally relevant question: Why on earth *should* one write? Is it necessary? Isn't it enough already to have lived through that terrible experience?

During discussions, various answers were proposed to explain the factors that might prevent Arab women in general from writing. Social and cultural factors: with family being women's main priority, everything else comes second. As mothers, wives, and sisters, women don't see themselves as individuals who are separable from their families and don't have time to write, especially if they work as well as bearing household responsibilities.

Written versus oral literature: We are the daughters of Scheherazade . . . Arab women's participation in written literature is relatively new, but storytelling and oral literature have much deeper roots. Women's historical role might be defined as transmitters/guardians of the oral social heritage.

Technical factors: A fear of the Arabic language. A fear of making mistakes prevents many from writing. This fear is related to the fact that Arabic is the language of the Quran and the sacred heritage.

Illiteracy: In Tunisia, the illiteracy rate stands at 19 percent. This number rises to nearly 40 percent for women in the rural northwest of the country, which means many women never even come into contact with the literary scene.

Economic factors: While the unemployment rate for male university graduates is 18 percent, for women it is around 39 percent, which means that simply earning a living is at the forefront of many women's lives. It's often said that women must have more time on their hands than men, but in reality, educated women tend to bear multiple responsibilities, including caring for children and the elderly, and can be considered the bedrock of an economy that depends on domestic labor—a contribution that is never acknowledged in economic statistics.

## What about Women Political Prisoners?

Let's suppose that a woman political prisoner wants to write, but there are things making her task harder or preventing her altogether. There are all sorts of factors, both general and personal; as well as all the issues facing women in general, there are the specific circumstances facing former political prisoners.

The participants all confirmed that family was their main reason for not writing. The following is a summary of what they told me: former prisoners avoid drawing attention to themselves and their families. Their main concerns are rebuilding family bonds, especially with children; ensuring the family is not at risk of arrest for reasons related to them; and trying to keep the family safe from harassment by the authorities, particularly in the form of prevention from work or restriction on freedom of movement. Women, of course, face all these issues when male relatives are detained. The family and family relationships are a woman's whole life, and she is prepared to sacrifice her own freedom rather than endanger her family. She is a "symbol of self-sacrifice for the sake of family, and she is expected to sacrifice." "The notion of sacrifice is associated with women, not men." I was repeatedly reminded by participants that "Arab society belittles women, unlike men." I was told of "women's humility and men's arrogance." That "women are too modest to show weakness" and that they "fear showing their emotions" out of concern for the label of 'ayb (impropriety)—a tool of control commonly used in Arab society—along with "fear of failure."

Then there is the desire to forget and an aversion to opening old wounds. An experience so huge, so painful, brings shame—especially when it involves sexual assault or rape. It often leads women to stay silent so as not to "tarnish" their family's reputation and makes them want to remain invisible out of fear that they or their family will be punished if they dare to write about what happened to them. Silence is a tool to protect the self and the family from harm. Meanwhile, different families respond differently toward female relatives who have been in prison. Several participants spoke of their disappointment at their families' reactions and their feeling that they didn't get the support they needed. In some cases, they were rejected by their families upon their release. Finally, some women are plagued by feelings of guilt, often about confessions made regarding other people or specific humiliating statements they signed.

Imprisonment, interrogation, humiliation, and torture cause psychological trauma; its longevity and impact differ from one woman to another. If writing is a beneficial healing process for some, others find it the opposite and opt for silence after their release so as not to have to relive their ordeals.

### Why, Then, Attend a Creative-Writing Workshop?

Bearing all this in mind, you could be forgiven for asking: What *did* make these women sign up to a workshop in creative writing? What did they hope to achieve by writing, when many were already civil society activists as well as working women?

The main impetus was the fall of the regime that they had fought against for so long and with it the barrier of fear—fear of being arrested, punished, or having their life made a misery. They are living in a time of revolution, and despite all its shortcomings, they enjoy freedom of expression and association. That in itself gave many participants the inner strength to face up to the challenges involved in writing and to refuse to be defined by the role of victim.

Participants wanted to write for all sorts of reasons. These reasons included the following:

- Wanting to document the experiences for the sake of "preserving the collective memory, documenting for the younger generations," "we write for our children . . . defining what happened to us, our history." "To throw light on what thousands of prisoners went through, from the *quffa* to administrative monitoring."
- "We write out of loyalty to the victims," "to keep the struggle alive, to tell the truth, to express and document our true feelings." "To produce writings that might be useful in lawmaking, or for other

practical purposes." "To be a better person, to be at peace with myself." "To preserve the memories of the women's movement." "So yesterday's victim can be today's active participant."

• And, within the context of transitional justice, "so that these crimes are not repeated, so torture is never again used." "To achieve reconciliation, communication, and acceptance of the other."

There was general agreement, then, on the significance of writing and the significance of documenting experiences; on the fear of forgetting, which weighs heavily on people's consciences—of forgetting a bitter experience, its causes and its effects; and on trying to draw lessons so that it is not repeated in future. But how? How is it possible, when we are aspiring to communicate with the reader, to convey an agonizing and humiliating experience in such a way that they don't stop reading, because the details of degradation and brutality are too painful to bear? Is writing about torture in all its savagery really the best way to communicate with the reader, even if to do so is an important endeavor?

Gradually, the question became: How, then, do we write our experiences? How do we narrate the events we've retrieved from memory, sift through for the truth, and document the cruel punishments that repressive authorities visited upon anyone who opposed them? How do we succeed in "writing about the unpleasant without making it unpleasant for the reader," as a critic once put it?

We also had to deal with the problem of the participants' differing abilities and capacity to master the techniques of writing and reach the desired standard in a short space of time. They had vast human experience to draw upon, but was that enough to allow them to produce literary texts that could be published in book form?

Here was where the intensive practical training came in—which, nonetheless, could never have succeeded were most of the participants not "in love" (their words) with reading and had they not already tried their hand at writing, in some form or another, at some point in their lives. They recalled:

"I began writing letters to my husband when he was going through the ordeal of prison, and what I couldn't get across to him, I wrote for myself. I felt like people were keeping away from me, and I didn't get any support from my family, so writing was my friend."

"Whenever I felt weak, I would write. It was a way of releasing negative energy. When I took refuge in writing, it would make me laugh or make me sad. It gave me a positive push. I can overcome the past. I write now so my children can read it. So I can live many lives."

"I write when I feel pain. Only when it stops do I stop writing. I've never published anything, because I didn't want to appear weak. It felt like being stripped naked."

"My relationship with books is like a fair-weather friendship. I only open a book to help me with my writing assignments. It was never about love. I read so as to do well at school. I tried writing some memoirs, but my sister found out and I stopped."

"I used to write plays. I used them to express my soul and my emotions. It brings me great joy to return to writing."

"I write in order to debate. I only ever wrote a handful of comments, about the invasion of Baghdad and the Palestinian cause."

Others threw down the gauntlet by confessing:

"Honestly, I've never been interested in reading or writing. I always just wanted to get an education, graduate, and be a help to my father. I'm here simply to record what happened to me."

"I've never written a thing in my life."

"I write in French. I don't know how to write in Arabic."

## The Process

My ongoing communication with the participants, sometimes direct but usually indirect—via my colleague Mériem Chaouachi from the International Center for Transitional Justice, who painstakingly organized the logistics of the whole project—played an important role in the process of the workshop. It also helped the participants' enthusiasm—which increased as time went by, sometimes to the point of competitiveness—for reading, revising, editing, and improving the texts after our exchanges. With time, the participants came to be close friends. They were brought together by a shared experience, harsh as it was, and were often moved to both tears and laughter. They knew all too well what each of the others had been through, even though the distances between them were great, the names of the precincts and prisons different, and their sufferings diverse as they trailed from one prison to another carrying the *quffa* to their loved ones. They found consolation in sharing their experiences in an atmosphere of Scheherazadesque storytelling that brimmed with grief, laughter, and hope.

From the beginning, I focused on writing exercises that would develop participants' expressive abilities, regardless of the literary form they chose, be it a story, the beginnings of a novel, a journal, memoirs, poetry, or vignette. Through these exercises, we discussed the various basic elements needed to develop a subject or experience into an idea: time, place, the senses, characterization, the use of imagination even when writing about reality, and the role of memory. All of it had to be done in a language that avoided repetition, and an appropriate register had to be chosen for dialogue, too: Should it be in colloquial Tunisian Arabic or standard literary Arabic? What about a simplified form of the literary language?

Each participant read her text aloud to the others, and ideas were exchanged. We discussed style; we asked for more detail; we enriched the texts with quotations, or poetry, or song; we learned to be faithful in descriptions of events and other people; and we tried to avoid making the self a heroic figure at the expense of others. Gradually, the texts were transformed from testimonies that "reduced the experience to mere names, dates, and prison locations without delving into the details, associations, or emotional connections that made each experience what it was into works of literary nonfiction that would transcend oral storytelling by being published and made available to a wider audience." We might read about any number of women prisoners and their cases, but "we can only gain a true sense of them by reading their own words, which will enable us to see what occupies their minds, so we can truly comprehend the horror of the experience and the ways in which they managed to survive it." Writing about moments of human weakness is not itself a weakness, and the darkness of prison does not mean the death of hope.

The book is divided into three sections. Part 1 contains texts written by women who suffered the misfortune of having a relative imprisoned. Part 2 contains texts written by women who were themselves prisoners.

Part 3 is the testimony of one participant about her experience choosing a "path."

These women's writings bring us a step closer to understanding the pain, confusion, injustice, and repression they have been through and the questions that remain, in many cases, unanswered. Most important, these texts were written in the full understanding that the aim of writing is neither to gain revenge nor to seek absolution, but to find healing through sharing truth with others.

### The *Quffa*

The *quffa*, plural *quffat* or *qufaf*, is a basket fashioned out of palm fronds or plastic and used for carrying small items. Commonly used in Tunisia, the word is synonymous with the basket of vegetables, fruit, and meat that the head of the household brings home daily or weekly from the local market, but it also carries negative connotations, thanks to its association with cases of corruption and appeasement: the *quffa* is what a bribe, often food exchanged for services or favoritism, is carried in.

Hela Boujnah, a human rights and transitional justice activist, says:

> The *quffa* has a powerful symbolism in Tunisia thanks to its deep-rootedness in the culture and everyday use. The expressions "*quffa* porter" and "carrying the *quffa*," for example, are used to refer to Tunisians supportive of the old regime who took it upon themselves to slander and report on their neighbors, friends and families to the dictatorship's security services in exchange for privileges and benefits, financial or otherwise, and whose actions led to violations of the rights of a great many people. Yet the *quffa* also represents another story in the collective memory, connoting suffering, sacrifice, strength and the struggle to stay alive.[4]

Najet Gabsi reminds us what the *quffa* means to the prisoner. "For me personally, the *quffa* was a mailman delivering my family's love and care,

---

4. This section is an excerpt from the text accompanying the exhibition "Voices of Memory," organized by the International Center for Transitional Justice and the University of Birmingham and held over three months in Tunis, Sfax, El Kef, and Redeyef that documented the experiences of Tunisian women through the motif of the *quffa*.

and a symbol of my dignity inside prison; I had no idea at the time what a burden it was for my family."

The suffering of families is hardly less than that of their imprisoned and detained relatives. Prison visits are a weekly torture endured by hundreds of Tunisian families: grueling journeys, hours of waiting, the expense of putting together the *quffa*, and the verbal violence of officials who enjoy rifling through the *quffa*'s contents on the pretext of a security inspection. The *quffa*, more than just a bag of things prisoners need, is a "bridge that links them to the outside world," in the words of Khadija Salah. Hana Abdouli is intimately familiar with the experience of the many families who had a relative imprisoned for their ideas or political views and who trekked from one prison to another to bring them the *quffa*. She says:

> It represents the warmth of family that a prisoner misses—the company they've been robbed of, the humor and the carefree laughter of relatives—much more than just food for an empty stomach or clothing to keep out the damp cold of the cell walls. It's the compassion of the grieving mother, the pained wife, or the anguished son. The *quffa* is the longing for freedom, the yearning to break through walls, the dream of escape from pain, defeat, and humiliation. And because it is so central to the life of one generation, it must be communicated by all means possible to younger generations, in order to document the dictatorship and its crimes against the physical and psychological dignity of the human, and in order not to forget the suffering of those who were oppressed, so that humanity remain united in the face of any threat to freedom—no matter whose freedom it may be.

# Salt Journals

# Introduction

*Writing Pain: Decrying Injustice in "Salt Journals"*

Brinda J. Mehta

> Prison is for the brave.
> —Najet Gabsi, "Hot Water"

Najet Gabsi's assertion about the courage, strength, and determination needed to survive the ordeal of incarceration as a political prisoner in Tunisia's prison complex sets the tone for the seventeen short stories and one testimonial that constitute *Salt Journals*. Written by former women political detainees who were imprisoned under the regimes of Prime Minister Habib Bourguiba (1956–87) and (ousted) President Zine El Abidine Ben Ali (1989–2011), these stories capture the horrors of prisoner abuse, sexualized violence against female inmates, the political and moral corruption of the state, dictatorship, and the socioeconomic disenfranchisement of the people. Both leaders were responsible for the brutal suppression of political dissent leading to the incarceration of thousands of political activists and labor unionists wrongfully accused of sedition by the Tunisian state. The peaceful Jasmin Revolution of January 14, 2011, that led to Ben Ali's downfall resulted in the amnesty of political prisoners by interim president Foued Mebazaa (*France 24* 2011). The political release of intellectuals and cultural artists led to a corresponding liberation of their cultural and literary productivity in the form of prison memoirs, protest songs, activist art, poetry, and testimonials.

*Salt Journals* is part of this literary corpus. The volume is divided into three sections. Part 1, titled "Here I See," includes stories that highlight

1

the impact of incarceration on family members. It focuses on the anguish of parents, the trauma of children, and the economic impact of prison on family life when the breadwinner is jailed for their political beliefs and actions. Part 2, "I Still Long for Daylight," describes the actual experience of incarceration suffered by the authors themselves. These narratives focus on harrowing descriptions of torture and other forms of sexual violence, the dehumanization of inmates and the suppression of their human rights, the trauma of imprisonment and confinement, and the resistance to subjugation. Part 3, "Testimony: Tunisia in Color," includes a testimonial narrative that charts the road to peace and freedom. The authors, who are all formerly incarcerated political activists, choose creative writing as a medium to document their experiences in an uncensored free-writing form that permits self-expression without inhibition. The prison experience shapes their politicized short stories that expose and denounce state authoritarianism and social injustice. At the same time, these writings express the women's intimate thoughts, emotions, acts of courage, and endurance in creative form. Structured as creative nonfictional accounts of prison life, the short stories offer the reader intimate insights into the women's ordeals; their trials and tribulations are crafted in salt-coated narratives of suffering, courage, and hope. As a life-sustaining element, salt provides the basic ingredient to flavor the different stories that emerge from a locus of pain and resistance: "Creativity is born out of pain" (see page 116). The women cry salty tears of grief as they narrate their tortured lives in text: "Stories are also a way to work through and work out trauma. Expressing the worst of life through storytelling also ensures a truth can be told," argue Hartman and Abisaab (2022, 1). At the same time, the very act of inscribing pain on the printed page generates tears of relief as a form of physical and psychological catharsis: "I have only one friend and savior: my pen, whose letters and lines create forms that become new forms and take me to a supportive place of comfort and harmony" (see page 117).

Writing pain is an attempt to heal from the traumas of incarceration, on the one hand. On the other hand, the very act of reliving these traumas in creative fiction is comparable to the pouring of salt on bleeding wounds to demonstrate how these stories follow the dual movement of "writing *in* flesh" and "writing *the* flesh." The narrative art of "writing in flesh" characterizes these blood-inscribed stories that emanate from the women's carceral wounds. Assia Djebar describes this writing as *sang-écriture* (1995, 275), or blood writing, in which blood replaces ink as a medium of expression. The bloodied hues of these stories highlight the intensity of the women's prison experiences and the visceral impact of the sexualized violence they confront in these carceral spaces. Narratives written in flesh are a means to write the body in textual form by giving voice and visibility to the horror they endured. These creative synergies between the "body-as-text" and the "text-as-body" represent a form of embodiment enshrining the women's voices against silence in textual form. This textuality eludes erasure, misrepresentation, and negation through blood writing's enduring imprint in words. The stories contest the culture of silence that has shrouded women's prison narratives: "I found to my surprise that not one woman had written about her prison experience" (Zangana 2025, x). The women have either remained silent or been silenced for several political, societal, and familial reasons that include the imposition of patriarchal morality codes of shame, the protection of family members, a lack of confidence in one's own power of self-expression, political intimidation by the state, and the gendered relegation of free expression and political protest to the invisibility of private space. *Salt Journals* represents a bold "coming-out" event in which the women unmask the hidden and forbidden aspects of their time before, during, and after incarceration in creative writing.

The stories in *Salt Journals* are motivated by the women's need to reclaim their humanity through self-representation. They claim agency as speaking/writing subjects to counter the anonymity and dehumanization they suffer at the hands of prison wardens who "tore away my humanity and my motherhood" (Mezghani 2025, 91). Stripped of their identity and their basic human rights, the women turn to storytelling as an important medium to write their negated lives into existence through what I term "word power." They attempt to speak truth to power in their own voices through creative acts of narrating, resisting, and indicting injustice: "I write to affirm that writing is one of the most powerful ways of conveying truth" (see page 115). The women use words as their nonviolent weapons of truth seeking when recounting the militarized violence of the state and its nefarious prison system. Their creative denunciation of state repression is a highly dissident act aimed at regaining control of their brutalized lives in strongly worded prose that also functions as personalized testimonies against the criminality of the state: "There was no justification for the crimes of the regime" (Toumi 2025, 99). The intrinsic link between creativity and dissidence in the uncovering of truth is highlighted by the late Dr. Nawal El Saadawi, a former political detainee, writer, and human rights activist from Egypt. El Saadawi equates writing with the revolutionary act of fighting: "Creativity is not only writing but writing and fighting for justice, freedom, love, peace" (2008, n.p.). Taking a similar stand, the authors of *Salt Journals* embrace El Saadawi's call to write and fight when they use the written word to create their own "truth and reconciliation" testimonials that bear witness to the ignominy of the Tunisian state.

### The *Quffa*: A Basket of Stories

*Salt Journals* is structured as a collective weaving of stories in three parts. The different sections are threaded together symbolically by the interlaced palm fronds of a wicker basket known as a *quffa*, "a basket fashioned out of palm fronds or plastic and used for carrying small items. Commonly used in Tunisia, the word is synonymous with the basket of vegetables, fruit, and meat that the head of the household brings home daily or weekly from the local market" (Zangana 2025, xviii). The *quffa* is as essential to daily life as the stories are vital to the women's existence; both are sources of physical nourishment and psychological well-being. While the market foods protect the body from malnutrition and hunger, the stories nourish the women's spirits against trauma and depression. By providing the basic narrative framework of the stories, the *quffa* motif engenders life-sustaining accounts of individual and collective suffering, courage, and survival, just as the market-bought meat, fruits, and vegetables sustain existence through appetizing dishes flavored with salt. In *Salt Journals*, the *quffa* represents a hamper filled with the women's memories of prison life, a basket created by the enduring power of "memory work" as a deep engagement with the past. These stories are nevertheless tempered by the grainy texture of salt in a briny aftertaste conditioned by the bitterness of remembering.

The *quffa* represents both a site of memory and a source of creative inspiration as the women detainees recall the pleasure of receiving a precious basket of home-cooked food in prison: "For me personally, the *quffa* was a mailman delivering my family's love and care, and a symbol of my dignity inside prison; I had no idea at the time what a burden it was for my family" (Zangana 2025, xviii–xix). Carefully prepared food by a devoted family member restores a prisoner's sense of self-worth through this personalized labor of love, just as the stories created by equally attentive authors reciprocate this act of love in narrative form. The delivery of the *quffa* to the prison is a perilous act involving arduous travel from home to prison site, difficult negotiations with prison personnel, humiliation of family members by prison guards, and other obstacles that impede the basket's safe passage. In a similar fashion, the crafting of these stories is a painful journey from inception to execution. The violence of memory obstructs the safe routing of these narratives through the trauma of remembering agonizing events, even as the women seek healing from trauma by writing out their experiences.

The *quffa* must be delivered safely as it is a vital medium of communication with the outside world and a lifeline of familial connections: "It represents the warmth of family that a prisoner misses—the company they've been robbed of, the humor and the carefree laughter of relatives—much more than just food for an empty stomach. . . . It's the compassion of the grieving mother, the pained wife, or the anguished son" (Zangana 2025, xix). Mothers, wives, and children convey the depths of their emotions of pain and anguish through lovingly prepared meals. The authors of *Salt Journals* convey similar emotions of grief and distress in acts of narrative solidarity with their families as their memories of incarceration evoke equally painful emotions, "the longing for freedom, the yearning to break through walls, the dream of escape from pain, defeat, and humiliation" (Zangana 2025, xix). The yearning for freedom situates writing as a highly political and denunciatory act "in order to document the dictatorship and its crimes against the physical and psychological dignity of the human" (Zangana 2025, xix). Similarly, the delivery of the food-filled *quffa* to the prison gate represents a family's defiant refusal to give up hope for the eventual release of loved ones. Salt is the common ingredient that links writing and fighting. The politicized act of cooking wholesome food to eliminate starvation and other forms of deprivation in prison—"my husband would embrace me through my cooking" (Ben Abid 2025, 50)—provides the inspiration for the "cooking" of these stories that bear witness to prison abuse in documented form, "in order not to forget the suffering of those who were oppressed" (Zangana 2025, xix). Salt provides the medium to season the women's mixed emotions that vacillate between "optimism and despair . . . a silent sorrow mixed with a timid, concealed hope" as they reflect on their ordeals (Mezghani 2025, 84).

In its physical and metaphorical configurations, the *quffa* represents a potent symbol of personal and collective resistance to tyranny and the suppression of rights. The multilayered intricacy of its intertwining palm fronds contains secret messages of love and hope sent by family members to inmates: "The *quffa* was always with me as I went from prison to prison, and I fought every obstacle so as to bring him my dreams and my affection" (Ben Abid 2025, 49). The sharing of secrets between a husband and wife through the mediating presence of the *quffa* restores the intimacy of their broken communication outside prison walls and prison bars by resurrecting the promise of a shared life beyond incarceration. Similarly, the coded secrets of the prison represented by its concealed torture chambers and inhumane treatment of detainees receive public exposure in the *quffa*-inspired configuration of the short stories likened to "a basket of torment and pain" (Ben Abid 2025, 48). While the *quffa* also has negative connotations linked to corruption and bribery—"the *quffa* is what a bribe, often food exchanged for services or favoritism, is carried in" (Zangana 2025, xviii)—this negativity is creatively transformed into interconnected testimonials of denunciation and a critique of the regime in *Salt Journals*.

## The Panopticon State

The stories uncover the conditions that create a carceral society when the writers describe the tactics of surveillance, punishment, and supposed law enforcement inflicted on dissidents by Tunisia's authoritarian regimes. Mounira Toumi compares Tunisian society under dictatorship to a heavily guarded "open-air prison." Laws and regulations such as administrative monitoring are arbitrary mandates to impose conformity and curtail freedom of movement and free expression even in the postincarceration era: "Administrative monitoring primarily targeted former political prisoners via their social status" ("Administrative Monitoring" 2025, 107). This law establishes unilateral state control over the bodies of private citizens through a series of exacting stipulations: "Administrative monitoring—understood as a form of state surveillance and control—was used at various points throughout Tunisian history to suppress dissent and maintain control over its citizens" (106–7). Such legislation creates a situation of social immobility through tactics of fear, intimidation, and informing aimed at promoting an invasive spy culture: "The police told me they know what we eat for lunch and dinner. Their eyes and ears are everywhere. They hear every word spoken in every town square" (Mabrouk 2025, 40). A society of informants is the basis of a carceral society in which every citizen is suspect and subjected to scrutiny by the state's internal security services as well as an unofficial body of informers, these "informers and people who were envious and resented our family" (39). The state's surveillance of inmates within the prison's private spaces on the inside is replicated by a generalized network of public surveillance on the outside. This vigilante-styled operation turns ordinary citizens into agents of the state through a correlated mechanism of spying and reporting. When the authoritarian "Father of the Nation" assumes the position of God in his omnipotent governance of the people—as revealed in the title of Mabrouk's story, "Bourguiba—God of Tunisia?"—the consenting citizenry morphs into dutiful avatars of the self-assumed godhead on the ground level in these overlapping systems of "subjection and objectification" (Foucault 1995, 305).

The dictator's mandate is serviced by the watchful panopticon, creating a culture of fear and submission within and beyond the prison walls. The stories uncover Tunisia's internal and external prisons that are destined to create conforming bodies; these bodies are reduced to a state of docility through routine punishment and surveillance in and out of the physicality of prison: "Fear seemed to have become their daily bread, the water they drank with their food, the air that they drew into their lungs" (Akkari 2025, 72). The indistinct boundaries between the state's prison complex and Tunisia's social complex under dictatorship, as highlighted in the above quote, reveal an ominous state of abjection, transforming individuals into Foucauldian "institutional products" that are beaten into a "non-threatening submissive 'normalcy' as the ultimate cure for deviance" (1995, 301). The ingestion of fear by the body leads to a condition of sensory deprivation or "submissive normalcy" manifested by choking and suffocating when fear compromises the body's operating systems. The deviance-compliance equation represents the state's ultimate dictum of "normalized" governance, denying basic freedoms to inmates and non-inmates alike in "the sharp blow of tyranny" (Akkari 2025, 74). The harsh strikes produce a series of societal concussions manifested in paralyzing symptoms of terror and fear. The body submits to the demands of an injurious state machinery of physical and psychological oppression represented by "three security agents, uniformed and holding the walkie-talkies they used to spy on the weak and vulnerable" (72). As a counterstrategy, *Salt Journals* represents the act of writing against fear as a survival strategy: "Perhaps my main aim in writing this piece was to draw attention to the aftereffects of repression. A regime may fall, but the fear it has provoked doesn't easily subside; it lurks inside everyone who has lived with its injustice. We must overcome that fear in order to live" (see page 118).

The stories reveal how the women ingest the noxious sounds and smells of prison while also rejecting this toxicity through their resistance. They compare the confining structures of the prison to "an iron box" whose heaviness is destined to crush their "broken and scattered" souls (Mezghani 2025, 85). The disciplinary mechanisms of the prison system are enforced through physical and psychological torture to beat the body into submission. The stories outline the horrific methods of sexualized torture in the form of rape, bodily disfigurement, and other corporeal punishment that are used to discipline the women for violating their gender-prescribed roles of obedience and compliance. As political detainees who have transgressed passive gender norms through active dissidence, the women become pawns in a patriarchal power game of body control between the state and its functionaries represented by the prison authorities: "My prison comrades and I were like lost, helpless pawns, shoved around by the hands playing the game" (Mezghani 2025, 87). As sullied objects "touched" by the state, the women are treated as sex workers through "permissible" forms of state violence destined to purify and cure their offending bodies. According to patriarchal morality codes, their bodies are supposedly corrupted by their active dissidence in nonsegregated public spaces and their gender-role nonconformity, on the one hand. On the other hand, the women are also regarded as sex workers "according to patriarchal 'tribal' traditions, chauvinistic interpretations of Islam and unreasonable societal expectations on women" (Zangana 2007, 117). These bodies-in-transgression must be ironically re-formed through a more egregious series of violations in prison. Consequently, body branding and corporeal disfigurement provide evidence of the state's commitment to maintain the nation's purity by manufacturing pure/nondissident/compliant women through punishment.

Rape and other forms of torture represent the ultimate "curing" of the female body through inhumane tactics of physical repression; these systems of violence represent the institutionalized language of unrestrained power: "One person's physical pain is understood as another person's power . . . because the torturer and the prisoner, each experience them as opposite" (Scarry 1985, 29, 37). Sexual violence becomes the most effective means to subdue the women through the fetishization of their bodies. Torture graphs a patriarchal map on the female body in the form of visible scars, lacerations, and ripped flesh, wherein the women carry the permanent imprint of these masculinist markings on their bodies (Mehta 2009, 40). Toumi describes the excessive use of force used against the women: "I would struggle to believe the excess of brutality, which ranged from beatings, insults, and humiliations to stripping women naked, tying them up and hanging them like chickens, forcing them to sit on bottles, and other preposterous forms of torture that were in fact completely routine" (2025, 99). Humiliated by verbal insults, hung like trussed chickens, stripped naked, and then penetrated by phallic objects like bottles, the women are exposed to an entire spectrum of regularized state brutality: "The torture is more attractive when it has a sexual component. . . . Rape and pain inflicted on the genitals are among the most common forms of torture" (Sontag 2004).

Sexual violence is an otherizing gendered experience that reduces the women to a degrading level of animality. Ironically, the state's animality against these defenseless women remains a well-kept secret concealed behind the subterranean walls of the torture chamber. These sites of in-famy are revealed through public disclosure in writing: "The night began to descend over the dark, foul-smelling place. It was an appropriate place for nightly torture sessions. Bats flitted between the cells. Voices rose and others fell. Sobs and cries for help echoed off the walls and rang in our heads, leaving us heartbroken and helpless" (Ben Hammouda 2025, 76). Tortured cries of agony and suffering are stifled within the impenetrable walls of the prison cells, ensuring that the state-maintained lie of protect-ing women from torture remains guarded from exposure indefinitely. The torture of women is consequently confined to the realm of the unspoken and the unimaginable. It is the ultimate taboo that cannot transcend the hidden recesses of the torture chamber. As an experience that is immea-surable in finite terms, torture-inscribed pain becomes an out-of-body sensation, outside the scope of signification and human articulation. The inability to feel or understand the pain of the tortured makes it an objec-tifying action for the perpetrator, on the one hand; on the other hand, the tortured remain permanently traumatized by the very "intimacy" of this unimaginable horror. Accordingly, torture underscores the power-inflected mechanics of the state while exposing the naked wretchedness of the condemned: "I was hanging from the ceiling, naked, my body stung by their whips. God, why now? Why tonight of all nights? Must the op-pressors crush everything, even the night of my dreams?" (Ajengui 2025, 70). Sexualized violence represents an all-penetrating infraction aimed at crushing the body's will to survive and resist. The state's classified "secret" (torture) dies with the tortured body, thereby eliminating any incriminat-ing evidence and accountability for this crime: "The irony is that the per-petrators of those horrors were the so-called security services. What kind of security could that be?" (Toumi 2025, 99).

There is no protection for the women who are placed outside the reach of the law for engaging in the "criminal" activity of political dissidence and gender-role defiance. Fatna El Bouih, a former political detainee from Morocco, explains in her prison testimonial *Talk of Darkness*: "Torture as part of a thorough search was permitted because we were *hors-la-loi* (outlaws). We were condemned before we were even judged. . . . It was not for what I did but for what I wrote. I threw tracts but I never threw bombs"

(2008, xii). *Salt Journals* provides confirmation of the system of arbitrary justice upheld within the prison system, comparing it to a farcical tragicomedy in which verdicts and confessions are signed, sealed, and delivered in advance of fabricated trials that reduce justice to a spectacle. Justice for these women is thereby reconfigured into injustice and violence through a corrupted judiciary that makes a mockery of their suffering: "It was a short trial, a mockery of our suffering. The charges were brought against us, and 'justice' was swiftly served" (Mezghani 2025, 86). Mezghani's story demonstrates how the term "justice" becomes a euphemism for the state's machinery of criminality through the nondemocratic intentionality of words and lawless procedures: "If you're ever asked about the judiciary in my country, tell them it's the scales of justice inverted and deformed, an arena of sophisticated brutality, a greenhouse of withering rights, a mill that grinds the disadvantaged classes to the bone" (86). Crushed by the oppressive weight of social injustice, the disempowered bear the full brunt of the law's wretchedness in the form of kangaroo courts and salacious verdicts. The judiciary represents the officiating domain of the state's "mechanisms of discipline . . . that makes them pass 'therapeutic' sentences and recommend 'rehabilitating' periods of imprisonment. . . . [T]he judges of normality are present everywhere" (Foucault 1995, 304). The judiciary's corrupt morality is authenticated and normalized by the state's equally corrosive governance in colluding bonds of patriarchal infamy. The stories in *Salt Journals* reveal the urgency to document these human rights infractions through firsthand experience while also serving as the women's only (and best) defense against the traumas engendered by the regime's criminal intent.

## Trauma's Landscapes of Pain

*Salt Journals* unravels the many traumas faced by the incarcerated and their families. Part 1 focuses on what I term "off-centered" traumas experienced by family members, especially children, who suffer the anguish of losing loved ones to incarceration. Nouha Dimassi's "The Girl Who Won't Grow Up" describes the inexpressible pain of a young girl whose mother is kidnapped by the authorities for daring to denounce the heavy-handedness of the regime: "The van and its passengers were gone, and I was alone, small, in a huge and hectic world. A world that hadn't stopped turning, even though my mother had been kidnapped." The story raises the following questions: How does a child make sense of the loss of a beloved mother who represents "the very center of my existence" (Dimassi 2025, 25)? Does society provide these children with coping mechanisms to bear this insurmountable loss alone when the world does not stop to offer sympathy and comfort? The story is an indictment of state policies that reduce children to a condition of premature orphaning when they are forced to confront the prolonged deprivation of parental love and support resulting from the disappearance and kidnapping of one or both parents. The child's recurring trauma from this primordial loss provokes emotional desensitizing as a coping strategy. The mother's prolonged absence and the girl's painful response to this continued state of dispossession lead to the loss of feeling and sensation, a symptom of irreversible and inconsolable grief. The child is reduced to a robotic state of emotional apathy and sensory disengagement: "I was exhausted by waiting, and I could hardly feel a thing" (27), a "nervous" condition that forces her to ultimately reject the mother whom she identifies as the very source of her pain. The child's psychic wounding leads to the "mute disarticulation" (Rivera Garza 2020, 7) of the mother when she eventually returns home from prison. The anticipation of future losses generated in and by this climate of insecurity culminates in the rejection of the mother when the child projects her own internalized pain onto her. In turn, the mother is forced to grieve the loss of her children in repeating cycles of rejection and separation that leave permanent scars: "Our hearts rejected her again and again, and we continued to hurt her even more than society had. That was the greatest pain" (Dimassi 2025, 28). At what point does rejection lead to acceptance, or is this damage irreversible? Do these forms of internal wounding ultimately lead to healing, and, if so, how does wounding generate healing in the absence of trust? The stories reveal trauma's multiple wounds while also offering possible clues to healing through the power of narrative: "There's only one route to the heart: via the word" (Ben Ali 2025, 54).

Trauma is both the manifestation and the source of the multiple wounds generated in a carceral society. Can a wounded society afford to remain in a permanent state of mourning without trauma's resolution in concrete form? Can the psychic wounding of a society's core being under dictatorship result in unassimilable traumas: "The story of a wound that cries out, that addresses us in the attempt to tell us of a reality or truth that is not otherwise available" (Caruth 1996, 4)? The stories demonstrate how the wounding of the mother by the multiple aggressions leveled against her by the patriarchal underpinnings of the carceral state represents a primary infraction. The mother's hurt is expressed psychologically in her lament for a disappeared son ("I weep and I cry for my darling son / I long to see him, but he's vanished and gone / I weep and I cry for that terrible day" [Abdouli 2025, 63]) and physically in the form of revulsion for the state ("She vomited repeatedly, so hard she practically puked up her own stomach" [Mabrouk 2025, 39]). The mother's physical and existential nausea provides the retching/wrenching language of the gut to express her unconditional dis-ease under dictatorship. In other words, the mother absorbs and dramatizes the unspeakable pain of incarceration as an idea and as praxis through bodily protest and grief. The violation of the mother skirts the realm of the unthinkable. This violence is symbolized by the tortuous wrenching of the mother tongue in a brutal suppression of speech and self-expression, a horrific act impossible to transcribe in words.

The most egregious violence is perhaps leveled against hijab-wearing girls and young women, as revealed in Chafika Ben Hammouda's story, "The Story of the One Girl and the Hijab Ban." The hijab ban was enforced in 1981 when Bourguiba issued Circular 108, "banning students, teachers, and public sector employees from wearing 'sectarian dress' in state institutions such as schools, universities, hospitals, and government facilities" (Anwar Munsir quoted in Ladisch and Yakinthou 2020, 84). The ban was reinstated as Circular 102 in 1986 and again in 2001 as Circular 35 when Ben Ali came to power. This interdiction denied the rights of Muslim women who chose to wear the hijab as a marker of their religious identity by curtailing their basic freedom of dress and appearance.[1] The

---

1. Muslim women political prisoners equated the pulling of the hijab with an act of sexual abuse; many of them perceived this violation as rape. They shared their experiences with Haifa Zangana with highly charged emotions and a sense of betrayal because secular-minded people refused to understand their trauma. Private communication, Dec. 3, 2020.

banning of the hijab delimited their right to self-expression: "This attempt to limit freedom of dress—and thereby, implicitly, freedom of consciences also—was never lawful" (88). These purportedly "secular" laws compromised the democratic rights of veiled women and girls by inhibiting their access to work spaces, education, and public service employment through undemocratic legislation based on religious profiling and discrimination (88). Ben Hammouda's story reveals how hijab wearing is considered to be a provocation and a crime against the state because it violates the tenants of "secularism" and its (antidemocratic) suppression of all forms of difference: "Since I was an only child and one of the first to wear a hijab, which at the time was limited to older women, my behavior was interpreted as a provocation to the regime" (2025, 75). The girl's young body is criminalized and targeted as a "body-in-violation" to be brutally stripped of all its protective defenses.

When the girl is brought to the Research and Investigation Brigade Headquarters in Nabeul after a house raid, she is threatened with rape by the security agents who await her arrival as sexual predators. She is instantly seen as prey in a convoluted sexual perpetrator-prey power dynamic. The very presence of her hijab authorizes the agents to aggress her publicly through verbal abuse and the threat of rape. Her hijab, as a symbol of dissent, denies civil protection when she becomes a disavowed (non) citizen of the state. Instead, the agents perceive the hijab as an invitation to rape the girl as they proceed to rip it off with violent thrusts and jerks. This simulated act of rape is a brutal form of unveiling through the traumatic exposure of flesh. The body is denied its dignity through the agents' conduct of indignity inscribed on her exposed flesh: "As I tried to recover, one of them barked at me, 'What are you trying to prove with this hijab? Chastity? We can rape you while you're wearing it'" (76). The tearing of the girl's protecting hijab is a forewarning of further violations in jail, starting with lengthy interrogations "full of lewd innuendo" (76) and ending with confinement in "a gray-walled, foul-smelling cell" (76). The penetrating odors of the cell bear witness to the repeated raping of women detainees, a dastardly act symbolized by the foul-smelling traces of the agents' putrefying semen. The vicious ripping of the hijab is synonymous with the sadistic wrenching of the mother tongue as primary violations against women in prison who bear the full brunt of democracy's hypocritical intent. This hypocrisy is couched in unjust legislation found in the different circulars against freedom of dress, administrative monitoring, and other laws that provide immunity to the state. *Salt Journals* represents the necessary corrective to expose and denounce the violent antidemocratic intent of the Tunisian state by reinstating the mother's voice in the different stories.

## Writing the Mother

The art of "writing the mother" in *Salt Journals* is a resurrecting act. Writing connects the severed mother tongue to the body of text through blood-soaked stitches that regenerate voice and script in a symbolic rebirthing of life. The mother is a force of regeneration. The voice of the mother, as "the first music of the voice of love," also represents the voice of dissent (Cixous and Clément 1986, 93). Dissension becomes the mother's ultimate language of love for family and country expressed in the unbending Ursprache "as a site of power and threat because of its associations with mothers and women's strength" (cooke 2001, xxvi). This archaic language embodies the voice of the mother who sings her lament in salt-encrusted narratives that underscore the association between wound-voice-text in memory work. As a form of corporeal autograph, memory symbolizes the architecture of the senses that awaken to the sound of a primeval cry, a birthing scream that enunciates creation-in-writing while simultaneously revealing the scars of ancient and current wounds. The inscription of memory in text corresponds to a particular birthing of voice that locates memory within a primal sensory consciousness that further reveals the ultimate connection between body and text (Mehta 2007, 14–15). The stories associate the voice of memory with the resurrection of the mother's wounded voice that initially manifests in pain ("it became a painful memory" [Ben Ali 2025, 55]) before assuming the force of plenitude ("I remember then the sound of her voice; it comes back in the darkness. That tone brings her back to life every time, the hoarseness that sends my blood racing through her veins when I hear it, even in memory" [Jrad 2025, 59]). The silenced ancestral maternal voice assumes its memory song tentatively in hoarse whispers and moans before gushing forth in pulsating flows of blood that animate the writings in *Salt Journals*. These writings are characterized by the fullness of sensorial expression moving from discombobulating suffering in prison ("my disconnected thoughts" [Salah 2025, 30]) to an all-encompassing state of expressive plenitude found in memory's scent ("The smell made the nine months of prison easier, wrapped me in the womb of its protection" [Jrad 2025, 58]).

*Salt Journals* emerges from the pulsating sounds, smells, and textures of the mother's protecting womb to take creative shape on the printed page, a testament to the strength and courage of its brave-hearted authors who represent the resilient women of Tunisia. Toumi's testimonial pays them the ultimate tribute: "You will rarely find a Tunisian woman who does anything against her will. . . . Besides, for someone to choose this thorny path, it must be her choice and a reflection of her own will, given the reactions and consequences she knows she would have to face" (2025, 101). The authors of *Salt Journals* will their stories into existence as a celebration of life after the penury of incarceration. They choose dissidence over subjugation, no matter the cost. These mothers and daughters of freedom use writing as the ultimate guidepost for their healing when they choose writing over silencing in their ongoing fight for social justice. The womb-like contours of the *quffa* offer the protective space to frame their salted stories that testify to the risks involved in speaking truth to power: "Dissident people liberate themselves from fear and they pay a price for this process of liberation. The price may be high or low but there is always a price to be paid" (El Saadawi 1997, 172). Similarly, the authors of *Salt Journals* pay the price of incarceration in their struggles for freedom. They use creative writing to express their individual and collective dissidence through shared acts of pain, resistance, and truth. They express their conviction and optimism in the future of collective action through their brave-hearted resilience: "The we contains the I and cannot be achieved unless all the many Is band together into a single we" (Jrad 2025, 57).

## Works Cited

Abdouli, Hana. 2025. "The Bread Intifada." In *Salt Journals*, edited by Haifa Zangana, Virginie Ladisch, and Christalla Yakinthou, 61–63. Syracuse, NY: Syracuse Univ. Press.

"Administrative Monitoring." 2025. In *Salt Journals*, edited by Haifa Zangana, Virginie Ladisch, and Christalla Yakinthou, 106–8. Syracuse, NY: Syracuse Univ. Press.

Ajengui, Hamida Ahmed. 2025. "The Happiness They Stole." In *Salt Journals*, edited by Haifa Zangana, Virginie Ladisch, and Christalla Yakinthou, 67–70. Syracuse, NY: Syracuse Univ. Press.

Akkari, Bouraouia. 2025. "The Night of the Police Raid." In *Salt Journals*, edited by Haifa Zangana, Virginie Ladisch, and Christalla Yakinthou, 71–74. Syracuse, NY: Syracuse Univ. Press.

Ben Abid, Hasna. 2025. "Hasna's *Quffa*." In *Salt Journals*, edited by Haifa Zangana, Virginie Ladisch, and Christalla Yakinthou, 48–51. Syracuse, NY: Syracuse Univ. Press.

Ben Ali, Jomaa. 2025. "The Heart's Path." In *Salt Journals*, edited by Haifa Zangana, Virginie Ladisch, and Christalla Yakinthou, 52–56. Syracuse, NY: Syracuse Univ. Press.

Ben Hammouda, Chafika. 2025. "The Story of One Girl and the Hijab Ban." In *Salt Journals*, edited by Haifa Zangana, Virginie Ladisch, and Christalla Yakinthou, 75–77. Syracuse, NY: Syracuse Univ. Press.

Caruth, Cathy. 1996. *Unclaimed Experience: Trauma, Narrative, and History*. Baltimore: Johns Hopkins Univ. Press.

Cixous, Hélène, and Catherine Clément. 1986. *The Newly Born Woman*. Translated from the French by Betsy Wing. Minneapolis: Univ. of Minnesota Press.

cooke, miriam. 2001. *Women Claim Islam: Creating Islamic Feminism through Literature*. New York: Routledge.

Dimassi, Nouha. 2025. "The Girl Who Won't Grow Up." In *Salt Journals*, edited by Haifa Zangana, Virginie Ladisch, and Christalla Yakinthou, 25–28. Syracuse, NY: Syracuse Univ. Press.

Djebar, Assia. 1995. *Le blanc de l'Algérie*. Paris: Albin Michel.

El Bouih, Fatna. 2008. *Talk of Darkness*. Translated from Arabic by Mustapha Kamal and Susan Slyomovics. Austin: Univ. of Texas Press.

El Saadawi, Nawal. 1997. *The Nawal El Saadawi Reader*. London: Zed Books.

———. 2008. "Creativity, Dissidence and Women." Roundtable discussion, "Creativity, Dissidence and Women in the Arab Societies." June 24. http://en.casaarabe-ieam.es/documents/download/124.

Foucault, Michel. 1995. *Discipline and Punish: The Birth of the Prison*. Translated from French by Alan Sheridan. New York: Vintage.

*France 24.* 2011. "Thousands of Ben Ali's Political Prisoners Released under Amnesty." Feb. 19. https://www.france24.com/en/20110219-thousands-political-prisoners-held-under-ben-ali-released-under-general-amnesty-tunisia.

Gabsi, Najet. 2025. "Hot Water." In *Salt Journals,* edited by Haifa Zangana, Virginie Ladisch, and Christalla Yakinthou, 78–81. Syracuse, NY: Syracuse Univ. Press.

Hammi, Mylène. 2025. "Grandfather." In *Salt Journals,* edited by Haifa Zangana, Virginie Ladisch, and Christalla Yakinthou, 35–37. Syracuse, NY: Syracuse Univ. Press.

Hartman, Michelle, and Malek Abisaab. 2022. *Women's War Stories: The Lebanese Civil War, Women's Labor, and the Creative Arts.* Syracuse, NY: Syracuse Univ. Press.

Jrad, Houneida. 2025. "A Meeting in Reality and in Imagination." In *Salt Journals,* edited by Haifa Zangana, Virginie Ladisch, and Christalla Yakinthou, 57–60. Syracuse, NY: Syracuse Univ. Press.

Ladisch, Virginie, and Christalla Yakinthou. 2020. "Cultivated Collaboration in Transitional Justice Practice and Research: Reflections on Tunisia's Voices of Memory Project." *International Journal of Transitional Justice* 14: 80–101.

Mabrouk, Soulefa. 2025. "Bourguiba—God of Tunisia?" In *Salt Journals,* edited by Haifa Zangana, Virginie Ladisch, and Christalla Yakinthou, 38–42. Syracuse, NY: Syracuse Univ. Press.

Mahjoubi, Chahla. 2025. "The Informer." In *Salt Journals,* edited by Haifa Zangana, Virginie Ladisch, and Christalla Yakinthou, 46–47. Syracuse, NY: Syracuse Univ. Press.

Mehta, Brinda. 2007. *Rituals of Memory in Contemporary Arab Women's Writing.* Syracuse: Syracuse Univ. Press.

———. 2009. *Notions of Identity, Diaspora, and Gender in Caribbean Women's Writing.* New York: Palgrave Macmillan Press.

Mezghani, Aouatef. 2025. "Let Us Celebrate." In *Salt Journals,* edited by Haifa Zangana, Virginie Ladisch, and Christalla Yakinthou, 82–91. Syracuse, NY: Syracuse Univ. Press.

Mgadla, Sawsen. 2025. "Fair Winds." In *Salt Journals,* edited by Haifa Zangana, Virginie Ladisch, and Christalla Yakinthou, 43–45. Syracuse, NY: Syracuse Univ. Press.

Rivera Garza, Cristina. 2020. *Grieving: Dispatches from a Wounded Country.* Translated by Sarah Booker. New York: Feminist Press.

Salah, Khadija. 2025. "Journey." In *Salt Journals*, edited by Haifa Zangana, Virginie Ladisch, and Christalla Yakinthou, 29–34. Syracuse, NY: Syracuse Univ. Press.

Scarry, Elaine. 1985. *The Body in Pain: The Making and Unmaking of the World*. New York: Oxford Univ. Press.

Sontag, Susan. 2004. "Regarding the Torture of Others." *New York Times Magazine*, May 23. https://www.nytimes.com/2004/05/23/magazine/regarding-the-torture-of-others.html.

Toumi, Mounira Ben Kaddour. 2025. "On the Margins of the Path." In *Salt Journals*, edited by Haifa Zangana, Virginie Ladisch, and Christalla Yakinthou, 95–102. Syracuse, NY: Syracuse Univ. Press.

Zangana, Haifa. 2007. *City of Widows: An Iraqi Woman's Account of War and Resistance*. New York: Seven Stories Press.

———. 2025. Foreword to *Salt Journals*, edited by Haifa Zangana, Virginie Ladisch, and Christalla Yakinthou, ix–xix. Syracuse, NY: Syracuse Univ. Press.

# Part One

# Here I See

# On the Slopes of Borj Erroumi

## Malika Missaoui

One winter morning, I carried the *quffa* and my son and headed to Bizerte
for my husband's 11:00 a.m. visit. Borj Erroumi prison was built on a hill
outside the city, difficult to get to without a car. You had to either take
public transit and get off at the bottom of the hill, then hike up, which
was kind of tough with the heavy *quffa*, or take the 7:30 a.m. bus, which
stopped outside the prison to drop off the prison workers and returned to
pick them up at 1:00 p.m.

I preferred to take the early bus and wait outside the prison. We were
allowed to enter the building only a half hour before the visit. My son and I
got off the bus and found a place under the willow tree, which seemed like
it might offer some shelter from the cold. There was constant sound as the
wind moved through it, and from time to time, the clouds parted and let
the sun shine through the high branches and I felt a bit of warmth. Looking over at my son, I saw that he was trembling, his lips almost blue from
the cold bite of the wind. The sea wasn't far away, and the place was quite
high up and exposed. I held him in my arms to keep us both warm, but
it wasn't enough and I started to worry. If he got sick, I didn't have the
money for medicine. I thought hard. What should I do? Walk up to the
prison guards and ask them to let us in? I hesitated. I didn't want to give
them that satisfaction.

On the last visit, my husband had asked me to bring him his *burnous*,
and now here it was among his clothes. I got it out to cover my son and
myself, but he was only little and he was so bundled up he wouldn't be
comfortable like that. I looked up at the trunk of the willow tree and found

the stump of a broken branch. I hung up the *burnous*, opened it up at the bottom, and held the edges in place with some stones, leaving a small opening to let in some light. We crawled inside the makeshift tent and sat down. "Go us!" my son yelled. "We made a house!" Gradually, his face began to regain its natural color. I felt warmer too.

My imagination wandered. What if I built us a little cottage out of some twigs and hay, like they used to do in the past? This abandoned patch of land was fertile. I could plant some vegetables, light a stove for cooking, prepare my husband's *quffa*, and visit him every week until he tired of me. A chicken could wander over from some neighboring field down the hill, followed maybe by a rooster. I wouldn't eat the eggs; I'd hatch them and raise the chickens. What a life that would be!

Life can be simple if you let it.

I was absorbed in planting, harvesting, and tending to my goats when I heard a sudden cry that brought me back to the present. I peered out through the opening and saw Lazhar, the surly prison guard, running toward us, screaming like some catastrophe had happened, "What's going on? What are you doing here?"

I smiled and answered, "God be with you, brother. We were freezing in the cold, so we made ourselves a tent."

He suppressed a laugh and replied, "A tent? You scared us! We weren't sure what we were seeing from up there."

He said it was only God's mercy that stopped them from setting their dogs on me and my son. Not without some pride, I thought, "Good Lord alive, is my husband's *burnous* really that terrifying?"

After the tent incident, they always let us go indoors while we waited for the visit.

# The Girl Who Won't Grow Up

## Nouha Dimassi

It all happened quickly, and events blurred together. The little girl remembers only the tears that sprang to her eyes (though not a single one fell) when she came out of the house and saw her mother being hustled into a patrol wagon full of policemen. She raced after the huge black-and-white van. All she wanted was her mother back. She would have given up all her toys, every precious or trivial thing she owned, if it had meant not losing her mother. She didn't want to be alone again. She'd been told her father wasn't there when she was born, because he'd been in prison too, for the same reason: belonging to the opposition at a time when such freedoms were unthinkable. Apparently, she was a good omen for the family, because he was released fourteen days after she was born, when he had been expected to spend the rest of his days covering the walls of the cell with the scratchings of his pen. Her father was free, but now her mother was being snatched away before her eyes!

She kept running. She didn't lose hope. She had to catch up with the police van and save her mother from those men. "If my dad was home, he wouldn't have let them take my mom," she thought.

Then my strength failed, and I tripped and fell. That child, three years old, running down the street, was me. Blood spurted from my hands and knees, but I didn't feel any of it. I was too busy staring at the van getting farther and farther away, taking with it my whole being, the very center of my existence. I watched it disappear and saw or imagined my mother waving at me from the window, like she was saying good-bye forever.

"Give me my mom back!" I screamed. "They've kidnapped my mom! Mama, come back! Don't go away!" No one listened and no one replied. People just looked at me in confusion.

How strange! How could life go on as if nothing had happened? People went on their way, and the kids in the neighborhood carried on causing trouble without me, like nothing had happened. I looked around. The van and its passengers were gone, and I was alone, small, in a huge and hectic world. A world that hadn't stopped turning, even though my mother had been kidnapped. I called out to her again, at the top of my voice: "Mama, don't leave me! Mama, where have you gone?" But my mom didn't come back, and she didn't reply to her daughter's calls.

That was when my throat choked up and I burst into tears, tears bitter with the loss of everything. My tears mixed with the blood that was drying on my tiny hands as I covered my face, frightened of everything. Crying was some comfort, because it was the only thing I could do, but the comfort didn't last long.

An employee came out of my dad's office (which was next door to our house), approached me, and closed my mouth with his large hands, so I wouldn't make the disgrace worse—the disgrace of a woman accused of betraying her country. He took me by the hand and pulled me quickly into the house. "The last thing we need is you making a scene!" he scolded. "We don't need any more scandals. Your dad's on his way home. Crying won't bring your mom back!" I kept crying until he raised his voice even louder and yelled, "Shut up already!"

I knew he was lying, but he gave me some hope that my mom might return. I took a deep breath and tried as hard as I could to hold back the tears. I think I managed.

I won't go into the details of what life was like over the three years that followed that day, which I remember like it was yesterday. It was the childhood of a girl without a mother and an outcast from a society that either wanted to avoid getting into trouble with the state or really did believe that her mother was a traitor to her country. The memories are obstinate, fading a little, only to reappear with resolute cruelty.

The days dragged by. I learned to rely on myself; I became closer to my siblings, and we were kinder and sweeter to one another. The loss taught me to be more sociable, to impose my presence, to acclimatize no matter where I was. I learned so much in the years my mother wasn't there. There was fun to be had, too, in the company of other children: kids from my granddad's neighborhood, cousins, and schoolmates from kindergarten and Quran school. The situation forced me to live a full childhood that was packed with emotions and with tiny details I was proud of. But it couldn't be anything but harsh to have an absent mother and an anxious father pre-occupied with his wife's situation. It's not that my father wasn't generous, or that we ever wanted for anything, materially or emotionally. He raised us well, wonderfully in fact, but he couldn't fill the gap left by my mother.

Mom returned on an evening filled with joyful ululations. I could see the happiness in the eyes of the people present. I was sitting down when suddenly there she was in front of me, entering with my father, her delight visible in her features, her smile, the way she held my father's hand.

We were no longer separated by two large iron-barred windows set at a distance from one another, as we were when we visited her in the various prisons where she was held, and my father no longer needed to lift me up to see her. I stared as people cheered and jostled to kiss her like it might absolve them of their sins and failings. Watching the strange scene, I thought: Where were they when she was kidnapped?

I saw her coming toward me, watched as her hand reached out to touch me. Her skin made contact with mine for the first time in three years. Her arm encircled me and pulled me to her, and in her eyes I could see the same tears I'd been forced to hold back on the day we were sepa-rated. I could hear her heart pounding as she pressed me against her chest. I'd waited so long for that moment: every time I'd been told off by an adult, every time my friends reminded me I had no mother. I'd waited for her at kindergarten parties, on special occasions, on my birthdays. I'd waited to see her on my first day at kindergarten, on Mother's Day as I clutched the gifts I'd crafted in class. I'd waited for her when my grandmother left us and then when my grandfather followed her. I had waited so long. When she finally held me in her arms, I was exhausted by waiting, and I could hardly feel a thing.

I was as cold and rigid as she was happy, and I couldn't respond to her, so I just kept waiting. When would she stop hugging me? I don't think she could tell that I'd had enough, that I wanted to breathe. She got what she wanted, while I remained frozen. I looked at her, thinking, "Why is she bigger than I remember—like she's not really my mother? Is that possible? Maybe they changed her in the place where she came from?" And, more important, "Why does she look so happy? What could possibly be making her so happy?"

When I look back on those days, I find myself thinking that what I went through when my mother was away, even though it was hard, was nothing in comparison with what came after she returned. Everything before that moment was bearable. The terrible thing was seeing my mother yet being sure she wasn't my mother. And even if she was my mother, I still couldn't bring myself to love her, to feel her presence, to respect her. I found myself living with a strange woman that my heart, sick of waiting, had simply rejected. A woman who was taking my place on the bed next to my father, while I was moved to another room, far away from him. A woman who competed with me for my father's affection and for the right to make decisions for the house and even interfered in the minutiae of my life.

The more she tried to win over her children's hearts—to do penance for a crime she hadn't committed—the more we snubbed her, even excluded her. Was it our way of getting revenge?

Today those barriers have fallen away, and my mother is my closest friend. I choke up at the thought of my mother wilting from the effort of trying to win my and my siblings' recognition, as our hearts rejected her again and again, and we continued to hurt her even more than society had. That was the greatest pain.

sometimes disagreed to the point of conflict, but we were united on the question of love for our nation, and the Palestinian cause was the main motivator of our hearts and minds.

We awoke one day in 1982 to news of the Zionist invasion of Lebanon. The Lycée was in uproar. We went on marches denouncing the occupier and the spineless Arabs. The Lycée was plastered with wall newspapers, which the students wrote and illustrated creatively with images of Jerusalem, maps of Palestine, and strongly worded statements. Student leaders competed in giving rousing speeches to clamoring audiences, urging support for Palestine, while cries could be heard of "Enemy, we're coming for you, from every home and street and neighborhood!" and "God is great, a storm to sweep away Zionism!"

I was one of a group of young women. Sana criticized everyone around her. Even today, when I try to place her in some ideological category, nothing really fits, but she was certainly deeply in love with Palestine. Amal's brother was an Islamist who went into exile during Bourguiba's reign, and she sympathized with the Islamist movement. She used to cry ardently when we sang revolutionary nationalist songs. Radiya was less interested in intellectual and ideological matters than in looking elegant; still, she followed our lead and always tried to stay close. She was the daughter of a former official who was among the great and good of our town. Sharifa was a carbon copy of me in her sheer rebellion against reality. Sharifa and I were among the very few dark-skinned girls who'd been lucky enough to continue their education.

We shared a love of Palestine and a dissatisfaction with the political and social state of our country, despite our intellectual differences. We nicknamed ourselves the "Naksa generation" and considered joining the Palestine Liberation Organization so as to aid in its struggle rather than just shouting slogans in the streets. We spent a whole week trying to make contact with the embassy of Lebanon before finally getting hold of a telephone number for the PLO offices in Tunis. We called again and again, but the line always rang with no answer.

In my mind's eye, I see my seventeen-year-old self. How I loved her! I felt so comfortable in my Palestinian keffiyeh, pants, and Tunisian military-surplus boots, with a Libyan Revolutionary Committees bag over my shoulder. The way I looked, it was like I embodied the dream of Arab unity that I've carried with me throughout my life.

I remember our English teacher Si Imad, who was feared by all the students. I have no idea why, but I wasn't scared of him—quite the opposite; in fact, I sensed that it was him who feared and respected *me*! He was an odd character, which the students said was because of some psychological issue caused by the blindness in his left eye.

Si Imad would pause in the middle of his teaching when I arrived late to class (which I did a lot) and say, "Look, Yasser Arafat himself has arrived!" I loved that comparison. I loved Arafat, and still do, because he was the figurehead of the resistance, God rest his soul. I guess my teacher loved Arafat too, and that was why he always paused so respectfully when I came in.

Searching for some inner peace, my mind exhausted by the intense repression of the early nineties, when members of the Islamist movement were persecuted—I was hounded out of the job market, kept under surveillance by the eyes of the regime, and summoned repeatedly to different police stations—I started reading different kinds of books, like translated Mills & Boon novels, Agatha Christie, and Ahlam Mosteghanemi's best sellers *Memory in the Flesh* and *Bed Hopper*.

### First Stop, Tala

I open my eyes and find myself at the first stop on my journey: Tala, a mountainous town that looks, when approached from the south via the Kasserine Road, like an open book where history has recorded its events. I have memories upon memories of this town of martyrs.[2] In early winter

---

2. After the revolution of December 11–January 14, Tala, the central western town, was given this title in reference to its martyrs. Tala, population about thirty-five thousand, lost more people than any other city its size during the demonstrations between January 8 and 12. The demonstrators in Tala were mostly young people. They chanted slogans that combined economic demands with criticism of Ben Ali and those individuals in power. The security forces fired tear gas, plastic and rubber bullets, and live ammunition at the protesters.

each year I'd wait expectantly for the white cloak to cover it, gazing out at the surrounding mountains from the window of our house, like I was reading the pages of a Mills & Boon novel describing the charming tableau of a British town waiting for the first snowflakes to fall.

I spent one of the most beautiful periods of my life in Tala, with my husband, God rest his soul. Meeting him was exceptional, and my life with him was exceptional. He transformed my life from perpetual sadness to never-ending joy.

We spent five years together in which I experienced love and embraced the feeling of femininity in its three stages: I was a mature woman at times, a teenager at times, and at others a child. I never imagined that a man could capture my heart, but that's what happened—and then in the blink of an eye he was gone. Without him, life carries on, but it is not the same.

I spend three days in Tala, then leave with my body while my soul stays behind, by my husband's graveside, in the house where my memories reside, a house I furnished with my emotions and sensibilities, and with the children that I had not physically borne but who gave me a sense of motherhood that I would never have had without them.

### El Kef

On the way to the capital, the public taxi stops in El Kef. I don't pay the passengers any attention, save a woman whose knee pains I share. El Kef's characteristic breeze punctuates our conversation and takes me back to another stage of my life. If I went through a list of El Kef's streets and alleys and landmarks, every corner would hold a memory. El Kef is home to the advanced college of agriculture where I achieved my dream of studying and earned my degree in agricultural engineering. I was only the second woman to obtain that degree in the governorate of Kebili, after Najat Belhaj.[3]

I spent three years studying in this town. Here, my political sensibilities matured, I entered the political fray—I was the first female student

---

3. Najat Belhaj died one year ago. She had more luck in her professional life than I did, finding work immediately after graduation and enjoying various promotions for her competence and skill.

elected to the student representative body, which we referred to as the *co-mité*—and I first came to blows with the regime, in the form of its security forces. I still remember September 30, 1987, the day I was taken with a group of female students to a security precinct for our refusal to remove our hijabs in conformity with Circular 108.[4] There they forced us to remove our hijabs and sign statements committing not to wear them again in the future.

One officer in particular caught my attention: he abused us verbally in the presence of his commander, yet when his commander left changed his behavior completely. He sneaked into the room where I was being held, while the other officers were busy interrogating my fellow detainees, and asked me, "Are you related to Ferid Chouchane?"

"No," I replied, wondering to myself why on earth he cared.[5]

He tapped me on the head with a newspaper he was holding, like he was reading my thoughts, and left. Soon after he came back and asked, "Do you know the poet Ali Lasswad?"[6]

"Yes, I've heard of him."

His face lit up with a glint I couldn't fathom, and he launched into a recital of several of Lasswad's poems. Was he trying to show me that even the men of the security services nursed a secret revolutionary fervor?

I arrive in Tunis at 1:30. I find a seat opposite the clock tower in Avenue Habib Bourguiba, not far from the Ministry of Tourism at the intersection with Avenue Mohamed V. As I sit waiting for my friend, I try not to look at the statue of Bourguiba. My country didn't have a revolution so as to bring back idols.

---

4. Circular 108 of 1981 outlawed "sectarian dress," that is, the hijab.

5. Chouchane is a football player from the South of the country.

6. Lasswad was a poet from Douz, in the South, who opposed Bourguiba's rule and was a follower of Colonel Gaddafi.

# Grandfather

## Mylène Hammi

My grandfather's house was dark. It stood at the edge of a working-class neighborhood in a mosaic-like alley with aged, crumbling walls, where the buildings had gotten taller and taller as they stacked themselves haphazardly next to and on top of each other. They seemed enormous to me. You can imagine; I was only six years old at the time.

I remember my mom had bought me sneakers that lit up when I jumped. The sight of my feet hitting the sidewalk, sending the colored lights on the soles blinking, often distracted me from her tears around that time. The sound of barking to my right disturbed my reverie, and I raised my eyes from the colored sprites in my shoes to the gray around me. I scampered quickly into the house, fearing the imminent thunder. I went into my grandfather's room, though his coughing annoyed me, and sat down on the edge of his bed. I sang to him, but I only managed to raise a smile. On his silver tooth I could make out the reflection of my own yawning mouth. A roll of December thunder punctured the room, pursuing me, and I wished I could hide under Granddad's white beard. When I remember him, I can still taste the licorice sweets he used to tell us were magical.

My grandfather died, and the magic sweets went with him.

I mostly remember the sounds of wailing and clamor from Grandfather's funeral. There were people everywhere, some of them crying over his passing, others harboring hatred and resentment—none of which I understood at the time.

Some people, like me, weren't crying. I felt reassured by their presence. The loud weeping scared me, and the silent people seemed like a refuge.

Later, I found out that they were from the security services; the people I had imagined running to were the ones to run away from.

I'd woken up early after a night of dreams, the last of which was about Granddad dying.

Mom wasn't there that morning to hold me like she usually did. She was grieving and depressed at losing her father, and the sight of the police posted around the house like chess pieces, drinking their coffee, made her feel worse. Some were even permitting themselves to silence the crying mourners.

It was the day of the funeral.

I later learned that my grandfather's last wish was to send a message to his brother, whom he hadn't seen in years. His brother was in his fifties and had been exiled for supporting the opposition, which didn't reflect well on his friends and relations.

"Don't come, even if I die, don't come. Let *salat al-gha'ib*—the funeral prayer for the absent deceased—be the link between us." He didn't come, Granddad, and he couldn't have come even if that were your final wish. After you were laid in the ground, eleven years passed before the revolution took place—and I wish I could've given them to you from my own life so you could have seen it. You wouldn't have had to die of grief over the work that was taken from you or the food stolen from the mouths of your twelve children by grasping informers. You wouldn't have cried in rage, wishing you could embrace your brother before you died.

I had a temperature, and the car, parked under a pine tree, was also sweltering in the feverish heat. I focused all my attention on the droplets of rain that descended in time with my tears. The gray weather added to the fog of my and Wahib's breath. Wahib was a year younger than me, but if he hadn't been there with me, I'd have fallen apart.

It was the day of Grandfather's funeral and burial.

I watched the men's feet as they carried the casket, swaying right to left like ghosts. The sound of sirens mingled with my favorite music; I covered my ears and hummed along, closing my eyes to escape the ghosts and the red lights of the patrol cars. Dad shut the car doors and left us at a distance from the crowd, not knowing that the crowd would inhabit our memories from that day on. The thought of death remains linked with the sirens of patrol cars and a song that I'm still listening to eighteen years, one month, and two days later as I write about my grandfather with a tray of licorice sweets next to me.

# Bourguiba—God of Tunisia?

## Soulefa Mabrouk

When the summer vacation of 1981 came around, I'd finished fourth grade with top grades, as usual, and won the district prize for best exam performance. But the best prize, for me, was getting to spend the vacation with my big sister in the city of Mahdia, where she worked for the regional government. My sister had a special place in our family. She was the first person in the family to get a government job and one of very few girls in our village who had.

My sister came home in late June or early July to take me back to Mahdia. Mahdia is a quiet city that lies in the embrace of the sea, which surrounds it on three sides like it's on permanent guard duty. The waves battle it out when they're angry at the harbor walls and tease sweetly when they're contented. We arrived in the evening at the taxi station next to the port. I was greeted by the searing smell of gasoline and sea salt, a combination that always comes back to me when I think of the city.

I was meant to spend the days alone in the apartment she shared with some other young women who'd been thrust from their villages into the big city to work. She warned me, I remember, not to go out into the street and told me she'd leave food out—my reward was the promise of a trip to the seaside in the afternoon. But I didn't get to stay and enjoy my vacation with her for very long. After a couple of days, only a few hours after she'd left for work one morning, while I was busy learning how to do some household task, the door burst open and my sister rushed in like a crazy person, racing around and hurrying me to get ready—we were going back

38

to the village. I panicked. Had someone died? That was the only thing I could think of.

Before I could ask, she told me our eldest brother had been taken from the house by the police and still hadn't come back. They'd accused him of being a Muslim Brotherhood supporter. We had to go home until things became clearer and Dad had figured out what to do. At the time, I didn't know what the accusation meant, but my sister's fear and anxiety told me it must be serious. She said he might end up in prison, and God only knew for how long.

Once we'd gotten out of the taxi and were walking down the track that led to our house, my sister fell apart. She was raving, blaming my brother for what he'd done, for blindly following people who were older than him, and getting tangled up with the authorities. I heard her say, "Why did he get himself into trouble like this, copying people older than himself who'll get out of it straight away and let him take the fall? And Dad's too old to run around after him in court. It's not like the regime makes it easy for people in situations like this. God help us!"

Next she blamed the informers and people who were envious and resented our family. Our family was peaceable, stayed away from politics and politicians, and focused on raising their kids and encouraging them to educate themselves and cultivate the land. Our dad had no connection to politics or its people other than the party he was forced to join, browbeaten by its local chairman into paying the membership fees of all the adults in our family once a year, and placing an inky finger on the ballot slip when elections came around.

The only politics our dad understood was how to deal with the land: seasons of sowing and harvesting, cycles of fertile years and lean. This knowledge resided inside him, and he smelled like the land and its seasons. He smelled like the soil embracing the first rain after drought, like fertilizer in a rainy winter, like spring when the chamomiles and anemone were in bloom, like the threshing floor at harvest time. He knew the land as intimately as a woman who left her perfume on him after every meeting.

My sister muttered and agonized and cried the whole way home. When we got there, Mom's state was no better. I was horrified as she vomited repeatedly, so hard she practically puked up her own stomach. The condition stayed with her for the rest of her life. My brother and I always screwed our eyes shut and ran from the room when she had a fit coming on, terrified she'd die in front of us or cough her intestines out of her mouth.

When Mom calmed down, Dad took the chance to talk things over with my sister. Lamenting the trouble our brother had brought upon himself and the family, he explained, "The police came in the evening and took him from the house. They said he put up a homemade poster in the mosque saying that Bourguiba was the god of Tunisians, that they'd made him their god. He's young—what's he got to do with all that? Then they said he was Brotherhood this and Brotherhood that, how should I know—"

"We need to get a lawyer right now," interrupted my sister. "It's pretty obvious they're going to keep him in jail until God knows when . . ."

When Mom heard the word "jail," she burst into fresh wails over her eldest son, whom (though she'd already had four daughters by the time she was blessed with him) she called the blossom of the family. "My son's life will go to waste," she wailed to Dad. "All that education for nothing!"

"What made him start thinking about the regime?" Dad burst in. "About Bourguiba? He should have considered the consequences . . ."

"I don't care if it's Bourguiba or the bey and the sultan!" shouted Mom. "Just think about how you're going to get my son out of prison."

"Calm down. Let's try to figure out what's going on first. The Lord works in mysterious ways. And watch what you're saying! The police told me they know what we eat for lunch and dinner. Their eyes and ears are everywhere. They hear every word spoken in every town square."

My parents agreed to hire a prominent and well-regarded lawyer who happened to be a neighbor of ours. My sister went back to the city. Dad planned to follow her in the morning.

I stayed with my family in the village. Whenever I remembered what Dad had said about the eyes and ears watching and eavesdropping on us, I imagined ears stuck on the walls and huge eyes in the branches of the olive trees, secretly monitoring our conversations. The ears and eyes of the policemen were even bigger. I imagined they could stretch all the way to the house. They must have heard what Mom and Dad had said about Bourguiba—whom we'd always been told not to mention. I was confused and scared. Our house was in the countryside, set among groves of olive trees. How could those snooping eyes and ears reach all the way out here?

That night, my younger brothers and sisters and I had just fallen asleep when I woke up in fright at the sound of Mom having another of her vomiting fits. I ran to her and found a relative of ours looking after her, trying to cheer her up and feed her from a bowl of soup that gave off a delicious aroma of spices.

"He's only seventeen," she said. "The judge won't take him seriously. When he sees how young he is, he'll realize he's been led astray by other people, and he'll let him go."

She was the first person to visit us, sneaking in at night, but over the next few days other neighbors followed one by one, coming at night or in the hottest part of the day when everyone else was at home, out of fear of informers.

In those first few days the house felt funereal, only there would have been more life at a funeral. Everything was imprisoned. The flock didn't leave the corral; there was no pasturing and no proper feed, just water and some straw tossed over the wooden fence. Several things died. The chickens squawked for help. No one had remembered to put out grain for them or fill their bowls with water.

One night, two policemen burst into the house and turned it upside down, going through books and anything their eyes and hands fell on. They still couldn't find anything to incriminate my brother. They left us and the house in a state of frenzy and fear.

After my brother's arrest, two months went by while we waited for the legal year to begin and a hearing date to be set for him and the other defendants. During that time my sister managed to see him and arranged for him to receive food, clothes, and regular visits. School was about to start, and it was meant to be my brother's baccalaureate year, so he decided to study in prison. I remember the day my mom visited him with a neighbor whose son was accused in the same case, taking all the textbooks he needed to work from. At home, we got ready to go back to classes, and Dad worked hard to make sure the four of us had everything we needed for the school year ahead. My brother's absence weighed heavily on Mom and the family; the doors of school and college were opening for us, while the door to his prison cell remained shut. It was nearing the end of his fourth month when the lawyer told us the good news that a court date had been set.

I later found out the judge really was sympathetic to my brother's youth and his earnestness. He'd said to him, "Wait until the mold is set; then you can do what you want"—meaning that he should get an education and secure his future before getting involved in politics.

But my brother made a special request to the judge at the end of the hearing that he be sentenced like the rest of the defendants, even though he had a lawyer appointed by the family, while his friends had only a single lawyer to represent the whole group.

That's how our men are: sons of the untiring women of our villages, they are nursed on integrity and dignity.

Luckily, he was sentenced only to one month in prison, and because he'd been in pretrial detention for four months, they had to release him immediately. He went straight back to school. He came out top of his year and got his baccalaureate and came in second at the national level in the 1982 Bourguiba Prize for philosophy.

There was one thing I didn't know at the time because I was so young, but found out later when I read his diaries: during his interrogation at the Mahdia security precinct, he was tortured and his beard was pulled out hair by hair.

# Fair Winds

## Sawsen Mgadla

I had finally decided to tell my family about my decision. I went into the living room, which wasn't usually this quiet. It always used to be noisy with my brothers' and sisters' laughter and my little brother's hilarious stories, but then we all went our own ways for study and work.

I sat down quietly by my mom so as not to bother my dad, who was engrossed in some television debate between two politicians. When the guests started disagreeing more vehemently, the anchor called an ad break, obviously thinking it would soothe the atmosphere, and I took the chance to broach the topic with my mother.

"Mom, I've decided to start wearing the hijab."

"You're joking, right?" she said scornfully.

"No," I replied levelly, "I'm serious—"

She interrupted me sharply and angrily. "No. No. Absolutely not."

I could see the furious disapproval in her widened pupils and slack lower jaw. She'd flat-out refused without even thinking about it. I looked over at Dad, expecting some support, or at least thinking he might emulate the anchor and try to keep the peace. But this time he kept quiet, and I even sensed some fear in his glances.

Mom found multiple and creative ways to say no. First she said it quietly, then she yelled it in a trembling voice, and we went back and forth, like an opera, the sound ringing in my ears.

It was as if Bouazizi[1] was still alive, like the revolution had never happened. I felt a new and unfamiliar grief, and I didn't want to keep arguing

1. Mohamed Bouazizi (born March 29, 1984, Sidi Bouzid, Tunisia; died January 4, 2011, Ben Arous, Tunisia), Tunisian street vendor whose self-immolation after being

with her because I worried about her health. I did as the anchor did and took a break to let the atmosphere settle.

I quietly retreated from the living room and went to my room, preoccupied with questions. Weren't we blessed with freedom now? Why this refusal?

In that moment of confusion, my mind raced in search for reasons, resentful of having to accept this high-handedness at a time when we were celebrating the return of our freedoms, though I also didn't want to make my mom angry. She'd refused, and I wasn't going to let that refusal stop me from exercising my rights because of a fear that was no longer justified. My wearing a hijab wasn't going to hurt anyone or infringe on anybody's freedom, so why should they stop me? I sought guidance from my Creator and prayed to him to help me, certain he wouldn't let me down.

I opened my bedroom window, and a gust of wind played through my hair, waking the past from its sleep, and I quickly tied back my hair to keep the memory in its place. But . . . I could smell it again, that same disappointment I felt at age ten when I was waiting for my aunt in front of our house. The wind whipped through my hair that day. My aunt visited every Saturday evening, but that day was different. It was unkind to me. I begged it to go on, I pleaded with the sun not to set, but it did and my aunt still hadn't showed up. That was the beginning of her absence, when I found out that she was fed up of signing in at the police station to prove where in the city she was going, and as night fell, something in me was extinguished.

While I was strolling in the byways of the past, the sound of the wind came to my rescue, bringing me back to the present. They were angry winds, protesting as my mind was protesting. Maybe they could hear my internal conflict and had come to help me; the wind blows from areas of high pressure to low, so maybe they'd come to try to relieve a little of the pressure inside me.

---

harassed by municipal officials catalyzed the Jasmine Revolution in Tunisia and helped inspire a wider prodemocracy protest.

At first, I didn't want to leave my room. I knew it was still there, still occupying their thoughts—that fear that never left us. Maybe it had won.

When the storm was over, I opened my bedroom door and went back to the living room. I smiled at my mom, apologized for earlier, and told her I was going to start wearing the hijab and that there was no need to be scared. As she looked at me, her eyes seemed to hold new depths. They were calm and limpid, a little confused and taken aback, but she quickly took a step away from her fear and worry for my safety and said, "It's up to you. You're free to do what you want."

I didn't expect her to yield so fast; I'd been bracing myself for a long debate. Maybe it was the kind intervention of the storm that did it. Sweeping through our hearts, it had blown away our fears.

# The Informer

## Chahla Mahjoubi

I get to work earlier than usual because I have a bunch of orders that need
to be delivered to clients. I start by tidying up, make a list of what I have to
do and when, and am soon engrossed in my work, racing against time to
get it all done.

At some point I stop for a minute to catch my breath and look out
of the window on to the main street. I'm suddenly thrown back into my
chair, like I've been knocked off balance by a heavy blow. It's the same guy.
What is he doing here?

"Hey, you and your *quffa* again. Where'd you get your patience from?
How come you aren't single yet?" That's what the man said, loudly, in the
public taxi that was taking me to Fatnassa, a village about twenty-five kilometers outside of the city of Kebili.

"What, should I abandon the father of my children?" replied the
woman, in a mix of disdain and defiance. The other passengers sat in silence as the conversation got sharper.

"What do you expect from him?"

"Why not? Why not? It's only because he stood up for what's right."

Their heated, fitful exchange got my attention. I was sitting in front of
them, and I turned around to steal a quick glance. My eyes found a pale-
faced, tired-looking young woman whose eyes contained a deep sadness
almost betrayed by tears that she nevertheless managed to hold back. Next
to her was a *quffa*. My own sister, her three kids, and her elderly mother-
in-law knew about the hardships that came with the *quffa*; my sister had

46

traveled the length and breadth of the country over the years, visiting her husband in prison.

It wasn't only my sister and the woman in the taxi who shared this cruel routine, but plenty of Tunisian families in the 1990s.

Their exchange was getting more heated still, and suddenly the man reached out and grabbed her headscarf. She managed to free it, almost choking as she protested: "Get off me, brother. Leave me alone." From the words she was muttering under her breath—"Dear Lord, this country is full of spies!"—I realized he was an informer who collected information for the police.

"You'll never get a job," another informer had told me on Election Day in 1989, all because an elderly lady had asked me to accompany her into the polling station. He tried to stop me, but I went in with her anyway. He knew I'd applied for a bunch of jobs, and he was on my case.

The informer returned to spread his poison in my life the day the district governor handed me the contract for a job at the trial court in Kebili. The appointment was conditional upon my removing my headscarf.

I'd been expecting it since I received the invitation to interview; the informer clearly knew about it, because he sent a girl I knew from the university to my house to accompany me to the interview, though she wasn't invited. I badly needed work, but I wasn't prepared to bargain. I threw the contract back in the governor's face, saying to myself: No. Not my hijab.

A work colleague's voice brings me back to the present. My face is wet with tears. I can see her lips moving, but I can't hear any sound. The voices inside me are too loud.

But what about the here and now? I look around me and think, I have to get this work finished so I can get home to the people waiting for me there.

# Hasna's *Quffa*

## Hasna Ben Abid

The *quffa* was given to me by my husband. He brought it back from a trip abroad, after the authorities finally handed over his passport, which they'd confiscated several years previously.

I took out the luscious fruit of all shapes and colors that were in the basket and carried it into the kitchen. My joy at the gift he'd brought me was troubled by the memory of another, different, *quffa*. Not the bride's basket, not a fishing basket, but a basket of torment and pain that was my companion during the years of embers when I used to visit my husband in prison. That time lasted from 1984 to 2011, off and on: he'd be released, only to be arrested again shortly afterward. He was in prison for belonging to the Islamist movement; they called them "special dye" in prison slang.

The task of delivering the *quffa* to the prisoner was one of the means they used to torture a prisoner's family and break their will. It presented two burdens for the family: first, the cost of all the ingredients, and then the time it took to prepare it all and take it to the prison. The dishes carefully packed into the *quffa* were ultimately reducible to their essential constituents of suffering and pain. But the *quffa* was also the fine thread linking the family to the son in prison. It conveyed a world of messages and feelings that spanned hope and pain, fear and optimism; it held emotions, scents, encouragement to keep up the fight, a challenge to the will-breaking machine. And it was always singled out for insult, inspection, and damage before it reached the prisoner. It was regularly used as a means of punishment, since it brought parental affection and care or the scent of a

48

loving wife—just as it was used as a tool of struggle during hunger strikes against the prison's injustices.

So I think of Hasna's *quffa* as something of all of these things. It goes in full, and it comes out empty except for used food containers and a few secrets. It tells me these secrets on the tiring journey home. They're messages from my beloved Lutfi, who's present in every line he's jotted down and every letter that's made it into my hands. I hold his words close and feel happiness and peace.

Once, among the things the *quffa* brought back from prison was a letter of apology from my husband to his adoring mother, which he'd stuffed into the folds of his laundry. It was written in verse.

Forgive me, dear Mother, for what fate has dealt me
Mother, I'm sorry, but my luck is against me
I think of you often on nights without sleep
As before me my path stretches thorny and bleak
The future ebbs away as each year goes by
It would not matter now were I sentenced to die.

His mother trembled when she received the letter. My husband was an only child, and I was his elderly parents' sole support. As their son's wife, I was their daughter, and I was all they had for as long as their son remained behind bars and couldn't have children. She cried and cried that day and asked me to read the letter over and over again. The poem brought a deep sadness to the surface, and she wailed like she was reading a talismanic invocation against the pain of separation: "My darling, my sweetheart . . . Even if I'd kept you in my heart, they'd still have taken you from me. What will I do? Men go to prison, but survivors come home, and you're no criminal or thief."

The *quffa* was always with me as I went from prison to prison, and I fought every obstacle so as to bring him my dreams and my affection. Making the journey was never easy, especially for a young woman by herself. I had to make the journey at night when he was in Grombalia Prison, in Nabeul, four hundred kilometers from where I lived in Kasserine.

I'd leave the house at ten at night to catch the bus to Tunis. The nighttime silence terrified me, and I hated being alone. On the bus, I always hunted through the faces for someone I knew, or looked for another woman traveling alone whom I could share the journey with, or found a family whose warmth and good company would make me feel safe and calm my pounding heart. I was scared at the thought of the journey ahead, and scared of the prying, mistrustful stares of other passengers, in the grief-charged atmosphere of the time. My biggest worry was looking after the *quffa*.

I usually arrived in the capital after midnight, when the bus station was empty. I always tried to be the last one off the bus, or I'd stay on board and beg the driver, who by now knew my face well, to let me wait out the rest of the night there. Sometimes he said yes, sometimes no, and sometimes he angrily sent me away, scared he'd be accused of supporting the families of political prisoners. The regime deliberately spread false rumors about us so as to isolate us and keep people away, and anyone who came into contact with us was punished, even relatives.

To get to the prison I had to change three times. The first time was at Bab Sa'dun, the second at Bab 'Alewa, and the last in Grombalia. It was a long ride from the station in Grombalia to the prison itself, by horse-drawn carriage. That day, as always, my main worry as I changed at each station was the plastic *quffa* and looking after the warm food—also in plastic containers, even though I knew that plastic was bad for the health. But what other choice did I have?

As I sat in the carriage, I kept my feelings of sadness and loneliness in check by looking around me. The road was lined with trees that radiated all the green goodness of our country. My heart fluttered with excitement as I watched them go by, thinking of how my husband would embrace me through my cooking. I was lost in these dreams, and we were almost at the prison, when the carriage suddenly lurched to one side, and in an instant the horse stumbled and the carriage threw us out, and with us the *quffa*, its contents now splattered across the ground.

I stood and stared at the food I'd spent days preparing, the dishes cooked just the way my husband liked them, mingled with the dirt of the road. It was silent around me, I noticed; the intense quiet filled me. Had even the branches of the trees stopped swaying?

I glanced up to find the driver looking at me pityingly, like he even wanted to comfort me. Something inside me melted then, and I pulled myself together. Wiping the tears from my face, I bent down to pick up the pieces of cloth and dust off the *quffa*, ready for the next visit.

# The Heart's Path

## Jomaa Ben Ali

It's pouring rain and the darkness slowly takes shape
Bodies become mere moving figures
The street itself is a side street whose every detail, every stone, every
    corner and angle she knows by heart
The place has acquired a certain intimacy for her since the day her
    steps brought her here a year and a half ago.

The face is familiar, unmistakable—slender and long, with broad
    eyebrows and a delicate nose.
The moment freezes, and electricity courses through her body
"My God, Amal, what's happening to you?"
She remembers he called her yesterday at exactly this time, from
    Paris, where he was presenting a new product
There must be a mix-up
But the captivating perfume Sauvage can hardly be a coincidence
    either . . .
"Watch where you're going!" yells a taxi driver.

A delicate woman raises her cell phone; its background is a photo of
    the two of them
The doubts dissolve into a burning truth
"Dad's waiting for us, love"
Her leg kicks against the bed and she jerks awake. Her pillow is wet.
The same nightmare again—it's been two months now
The nightmare is clinging on, but she has to get ready to go out . . .

*Remember how we used to walk, walk and talk*
*And now we're back like we started*
That's how Mayada Basilis's song has accompanied us throughout
our days.

We've taken many routes we didn't want to, but this time the route is
very different
The capital. God, it's crowded! Amal pushes her way through the
streets with "Excuse me" and "Sorry"
She's done with all these wandering bodies and all this excessive love
you see wherever you turn your face in the capital.
Amal has never liked its streets, but they've always held those she loves
She drags her suitcase along, and something wants to fly toward the
horizon
"Things will turn out wonderfully," she repeats to herself.

The waiting is over, the journey has begun
The route leads out of the capital toward lovely Nabeul, and
specifically northern Hammamet, which she knows well
She's done this journey three years in a row, but this time feels
different, like the first time
How long's it been?
A long time. To be more precise, since June 18, 2013, the day of her
graduation.
How time flies, and how the years age us.
The journey's fast this time, and the cars and the noise gradually
disappear.
The city noise finally dwindles to nothing
I don't know how a sane person can live in a big city like that, she
thinks.

Hammamet gets closer
There's a woman out jogging
Amazing!
Finally, someone running to cast off their fatigue—a woman running
alongside life, and not behind it

A common cold has tired her out, and she closes her eyes for a few
    moments
A short nap, a little cutout of time. The singer's wonderful voice
    comes back to her:
*And now we're back like we started*

She really has returned to Nabeul, to Hammamet, only this time it's
    to a hotel
Still, it's the same route, and there's only one route to the heart: via
    the word.
Amal's dreams took her to study English, and today the same long
    journey takes her to the language her heart loves best:
Arabic.

How do you get through this life? Which way is it leading?
The truth, or at least the questions, always seem urgent to her.
How often has she confronted her fears and taken the path she wants
    to take?
How many times has she found herself at the world's back door?
How many paths has she really embraced, loved the sound of her
    footsteps on?
It doesn't take long to get to the hotel, like all the times she's been to
    Nabeul when she doesn't want to.
She thinks about graduation day. She was sitting by the window,
    trying to memorize the features of the route in her heart,
    because she didn't know when she'd walk this road to her heart
    again.

Walking really did take up many years.
Nabeul, June 18, 2013; and today, Nabeul, January 25, 2018.
God, moving toward life demands more than we think.

I forgot to introduce myself:
Amal Muhammad, unemployed by order of the homeland
But how will the homeland ever accommodate our dreams instead of
    trampling them underfoot,

when things have been worsening since the start of the Arab Spring, whose blossoms are yet to be seen?

I'm also the daughter of a father who's faced every kind of political harassment.

I remember one conversation we had recently about setting right the damage and acknowledging the atrocities that had been committed against so many people, and what measures doing so might require.

We recalled, together, how our lives were turned upside down by a single phone call, how my father's office was confiscated, how we didn't see him for months afterward.

We talked about details I still remember, though I was very young at the time.

Dad's huge closet where I hid for hours after the break-in; Mom's anxiety.

I stayed in a state of shock for days, and it became a painful memory that couldn't be erased by the revolution, or the democracy that we took a few timid steps toward.

Plenty of listening and plenty of tears, but no practical plans for redress. Reckoning and accountability are on hold.

"Girls are always the kindest," repeats the elderly man in his seventies, my father, his heart bursting with life and defiance— far more than the youth of today

He's tall and imposing, with bright, shining eyes that see the world through the gaze of his three daughters.

His firm footfalls are heard in the corridor at every prayer time. The sound of running water for his ablutions, the footsteps as he leaves for mosque—these sounds tell his little family that all is well with the world.

Even those times when he shows his sternness, when his daughters say he's a dictator and it's just impossible to live with him, he can dispel.

The years he spent in prison took so much from him and changed him.

He wears a red *qashabiyya* made of thick coarse wool woven by his
Fatima, his life's companion, the lucky girl he'd waited for as she
grew up, and then married.

The red *qashabiyya* tells you so much about them both, about their
patience, their love, their long intimacy.

I never heard him affect any of those overdone expressions of
adoration that people use. Instead, he says, "Fatima, you are my
hands and my legs."

He is Hajj Muhammad, unchanging in a world that changes every
moment.

My father is a simple man who is close to the earth, who will teach
you to sow and wait patiently until it's time to reap

That was the same way he taught the principles of his religion, before
he was arrested.

There, in a village in the far southeast, in a small house, is a
mountain that doesn't age. A man who has devoted his life to the
love of the book of God, his three daughters and their mother,
and his two sons who went abroad

A man whose heart is orbited by three doves that tell you: a father is
a thing of heaven.

# A Meeting in Reality and in Imagination

## Houneida Jrad

Look around you. You'll see that ambient white light that is the sound of each soul whispering to the souls around it. That's where we begin. These voices you hear around you are the sound of pain and strength and hope: hope for a new beginning, for a sweeping away of the darkness and the injustice of the years of embers, for an unfurling of stars in the sky once again, for a sowing of seeds from which love will grow, for a new sunrise that will shine light into every dark corner so every soul will yield and every heart become calm.

Here I was, then. With the red chairs and the walls covered in clean engraved mirrors. On the other side, the wall was white, and two paintings had been hung on it. One of them caught my eye: a woman wearing the traditional garment called a *safsari*.

The picture reminded me of the women who fought. They were a refuge, a source of support, prophets even, in the lessons they taught us about how to be patient and steadfast and loving. They were our only link to the outside world when we were in prison.

When we fight for what we dream of, what we believe in, what we want, it's that "we" that matters, that accompanies our actions and words, our thoughts and principles, everything we've done, past and present. The we contains the I and cannot be achieved unless all the many Is band together into a single we.

When my mother used to visit me in prison, I used to eagerly snatch her handkerchief before I took the *quffa*—the basket of food and supplies

57

she'd brought—or even said anything to her. Mom was so tolerant of my strange ideas and requests! I used to make her tuck a handkerchief inside her clothes and not take it out until the next visit. That handkerchief kept me company, kept my spirits up, kept my homesickness in check. Through it I could smell everything that had happened at home while I was away. The scent of the henna that covered her palms never left me—even though I'd always hated it when I was young. The smell made the nine months of prison easier, wrapped me in the womb of its protection. Even after I left prison I was adamant that my mom keep her hands dyed with henna so I'd always be safe.

From the white leaves of paper where I released my sadness by writing, and defending the rights of the oppressed, to the green leaves of henna furled in the center of my heart—how is it that leaves can represent a country for someone?

My thoughts were interrupted by a female voice inquiring, "Excuse me, Madame Baya?"

"That's me," I replied. "I guess you must be the journalist that called me last week?"

The younger woman nodded, smiling and trying to keep a handle on her emotions. She'd been waiting a long time for this meeting, to talk to Madame Baya and to look at her, to memorize what details she could of her features, the sound of her voice. But she had to be professional in this interview: she wanted to earn Madame Baya's trust, to befriend her, and maybe be lucky enough to get another meeting. She'd turned up two hours before their appointment just to watch, from a distance, this woman, so renowned for her wisdom even though she was so young. What was the secret of her strength and pride and the smile that never left her face, despite that piercing gaze?

She'd known about Madame Baya since she was young. Whenever her name was mentioned, it would be in a hushed voice, she'd noticed, accompanied by a careful glance around to check that nobody had heard. That's what had first made her curious; that's why she was so excited to meet her now. She'd spent nights trying to visualize her, trying to picture her face. Would she have pale honey-colored eyes and long black hair? Or would she look like the women in the neighborhood, pale and heavy? She'd once seen a picture of Madame Baya in a foreign magazine, though, wearing her lawyer's uniform and raising her right fist as she marched with other lawyers against the regime. In real life, her features were both strong and gentle at the same time, and she was slim and not as tall as it seemed in the picture. Most eye-catching was the set of her face, which was plump, with a dimple in her left cheek and large eyes filled with a dreamy gaze. In the photo, she had been shouting so hard the veins on her neck stood out. The protest attracted a lot of international attention at the time, especially what with the persecution the protesters had faced in the aftermath. She spent nights talking to the photo.

And so she grew up dreaming of meeting Madame Baya and getting to know her. She used to peek through the keyhole when Uncle Azhar visited them in his long brown coat and black hat. Uncle Azhar worked secretly with her father in the party of which Madame Baya, too, was a member, and he might say something about her. Then her mom found her spying and told her off. The telling-off didn't stop her thinking about the brave and noble lawyer. And now here she was.

How can a single year bring so many events and people and experiences? Especially those moments that snatch you out of the light, where you were so happy, and shut you in a cellar of darkness where there's nothing for company but your own fear and weakness and everything you've run away from, and you know then that you're weak and you have no one to turn to and nowhere to go. At these times all I have is my imagination and the recollections that are strewn around the corners of my memory.

I remember then the sound of her voice; it comes back in the darkness. That tone brings her back to life every time, the hoarseness that sends my blood racing through her veins when I hear it, even in memory. That embrace that shelters me and sings to me of every nation in the world as if they'd been created for me alone. The limitless ability to love and give and sacrifice that makes me embarrassed to admit to the weakness or fear in front of me, because what I've been through can't possibly compare with what happened to her, not even in the simplest details.

It was she who held my hand and led me out of the darkness and into the light, where I gathered up what was left of myself and used my soul's resources to sculpt it into shape. She whom despair and fear could not touch; our coming together that year was one of the most momentous things that ever happened to me. Her door had been closed all those years, but she opened it to me, and through her experience I learned through everything she witnessed in all the places life took her.

We cannot be reduced to a single time or place, but only to the burdens we carry in our wounds, and what wanders in our thoughts, and what our souls dictate to us. That is how we shape and outline. That is how we watch, with the eyes of our hearts. Borders collapse; differences in age and experience and appearance no longer mean a thing. That is how our bonds are dissolved.

# The Bread Intifada

## Hana Abdouli

I was sitting with my friends on the balcony of our house. Something soft and soulful was playing in the background, and we were sipping coffee and chatting, breaking into loud laughter now and then, when I heard the sound of clamoring voices, coming closer. Turning to look out onto the street, I saw an agitated crowd approaching. I watched, and listened, my heart pounding. A shiver ran through my body and I began to succumb to fear. What was going on?

People were advancing from all the side streets onto the main road, and soon all I could see was a growing mass of black, the voices rising and gaining in clarity as they came closer, until the scene was complete before me: a coffin wrapped in the flag of my country, hands held up with the victory sign, the picture of a young man occupying a prominent place in the first row, and then the chants:

> We'll give our blood and soul for you, o martyr.
> With our blood, we defend you.
> You can rest.
> The struggle shall continue.

I was twenty years old when those events shattered the barrier of silence that surrounded us.

It was a mix of fear and confusion that I felt in those first moments. I had no idea what was going on. The sound of gunshots coming from the other direction—it wasn't clear who they were aimed at—didn't help. My friends and I, along with the rest of my family, stumbled indoors and closed all the doors and windows behind us.

There was a huge commotion. The sound of heavy boots could be heard on the roofs. The majority of the demonstrators were young men. We could hear them going loudly back and forth in the alleyways around the house, their voices never seeming to get tired. The chants stopped only for a moment when the sound of buckshot rang in the air, rising again as soon as the shooting subsided.

Those were difficult days, unlike anything I'd witnessed before. The clashes between the young protesters and the police continued daily and intensified whenever a protester was martyred or arrested. The power cuts continued too and the incursions of security forces combing through the entire neighborhood.

The picture from that first protest remained stuck in my mind. Who was he?

I later learned that it was Fadhel Sassi, a young man killed outside the Faculty of Arts and Humanities in Tunis on January 3, 1984, while taking part in a demonstration against the increase in bread prices, just one of numerous protests that had sprung up all over the country.

"We will raise the price of bread and flour," the president had announced on television, "because according to the prime minister, tons of each get thrown out with the garbage."

In response, people took to the streets. The protests spread throughout the country like wildfire. The city of Douz, known as "the gateway to the Sahara," saw some terrible events on December 29, 1983, before the events peaked on January 3. That was the Black Thursday when the blood of so many young people was shed. A week after the bloody events, the president came out with a second announcement revoking the first.

Thousands of poor people filled the streets, raising their hands in victory signs. As for the elite, they considered the outcome a sort of consolation for the loss of comrades and loved ones. Fadhel became a symbol of sacrifice, immortalized by poets of the free word in the song "O Martyr" (Ya Shahid), which is still sung to this day:

O martyr, o martyr
The bread is back, o martyr
Martyr of bread, revolt

A rose took root in your grave
Call to the people and they will come

When Fadhel was killed, his blood, like the blood of his comrades before him, nourished the homeland's soil. That day, he was wedded to the land that had seen his birth, cherished his first steps, and watched him grow up to be a man. He was celebrated in every region of the country, especially on university campuses, because students were the pulsing veins of society. Many of them came from deprived or forgotten parts of the country, where education was their families' only hope for a better future.

Once things had settled down, the night patrols went back to arresting young dissidents. Students were the main victims. Instead of reaping the rewards of their years of study, gaining their degrees, and going on to benefit the country and help their families, they found themselves locked up behind bars.

I weep and I cry for my darling son
I long to see him, but he's vanished and gone
I weep and I cry for that terrible day
When the jailers came and took him away
I'm told that he's been tortured and abused
At the hands of his captors, beaten and bruised

I can still hear the mother singing the words to her imprisoned son. Her face is etched in my memory, the warm tears that flowed down her pale, age-withered cheeks following the lines of patience and dignity in her wrinkles. She was separated by several meters from a part of her own self, the part that she had devoted her life for. Her husband's early death had left her the sole provider for two sons and a daughter who were as defenseless as small birds, and she did all she could to feed them and send them to school.

The image stuck in my mind: the mother on a visit to her son, trembling hands held out, trying to hug him despite the iron bars between them. The poor woman flung herself toward her son, ignoring the clatter of the dark iron doors and the voice and bulk of the jailer with his bulging belly. All she wanted at that moment, all she had been dreaming of, was for her son to bury his head in her arms so she could pull him close and breathe in his smell.

# Part Two
# I Still Long for Daylight

# The Happiness They Stole

## Hamida Ahmed Ajengui

We stopped in front of the big white house. My brother leaned on the car horn to alert the people in the house that we'd arrived, then turned to me and asked, "When will you be ready?" I answered, "Eight p.m., I think."

The young woman who opened the door had a huge smile that lit up her face. She was waiting for me. It was Faiza, my friend and hairdresser. My brother took my wedding dress out of the car and brought it in.

It was the twentieth day of the seventh month of the ninety-sixth year of the twentieth century, the day I was going to be a bride, after five long years of waiting for my absent love. My dream was finally coming true, and I wasn't going to let anyone take it away from me.

The hair salon occupied a corner in the garden of the big house. Faiza gestured to a beautiful red couch and told me to make myself comfortable. I stretched myself out in the morning sun, grateful for some rest. I hadn't been able to relax all week, since the wedding preparations began, especially with my father still persisting in opposing my marriage to Hassib.

Hassib was a handsome young man who had come to the capital from faraway Kairouan, having been expelled from his college for taking part in the Bread Intifada.[1] He came to live here, and we became neighbors. I admired his manners and intellect and became attached to him.

---

1. Also known as the Tunisian bread riots, a series of demonstrations that took place in various Tunisian cities between December 1983 and January 1984, triggered by a rise in the price of bread owing to an austerity program imposed by the International Monetary Fund.

His family circumstances forced him to rely on himself while he was a student. He studied in the morning and worked in the evening. He loved to write, and every time he gave me one of his texts to read, I fell in love with him a little more. The difficulties of the times meant we couldn't get to know each other properly. Couples used to come to the capital to escape their families and snatch some time together. We, on the other hand, would take the bus downtown, not for a romantic date, but to take part with hundreds of other young people in protests demanding freedom of expression—which always ended in the police chasing protesters and turning working-class neighborhoods upside down in search of participants.

Hassib and I were among the thousands who got arrested in 1991. Prison kept our bodies apart but brought our hearts closer together. Letters were delivered to the central prison from other prisons around the country, where prisoners were held as part of a strategy of "prison tourism" that was an additional punishment to prisoners and their families, who got poorer and wearier with every trip north or south to see their loved ones.

The letters came to me regularly. I received them from the hands of the kindhearted prison guard Hadda, who was charged with reading incoming and outgoing letters. She used to bang on the door of the cell and bellow, "Letter for you, Hamida. You and your fiancé are ruining my eyesight. Tell him to make his handwriting a bit bigger!" Then she'd laugh and walk away.

My cellmates would tease me and snatch the letter out of my hands. In tiny handwriting, Hassib filled every corner of every page with words carrying hope and the dream of a better future.

After my release from prison, my father started to intercept the postman, and most of my letters ended up in the pocket of his coat. My mother faced him patiently as he fumed, "Her rebelliousness is his fault. I've always said that," and I listened in my room and cried. It was another two whole years of waiting until Hassib was out of prison. Hassib didn't let me down. Immediately after his release in 1996, he came to our house with his mother and pleaded with my father and brothers for my hand in marriage. My father eventually relented, thanks to my older uncle's mediation, but not without making a series of exaggerated, crippling demands that he was certain Hassib would fail to meet. The exact opposite happened: Hassib took it as a challenge and spent all his savings to provide everything my father asked him for. The tension wasn't over, though. My father's temper worsened as the wedding drew near. I know it was all out of concern for my safety; he wanted to shield me from the daily torment of police surveillance. He couldn't bear the idea of my pain and suffering. He foresaw what the future might bring and kept asking, "What will their life be like when they're both in the same kind of trouble?"

The bright sunlight streaming through the window brought me back from my ruminations. Faiza was busy preparing the makeup and accessories. "I let you rest for a bit, but we can start now if you like. We're kind of running out of time," she said.

After a few hours under Faiza's expert hands, I was looking in the mirror at a truly beautiful bride, glowing in a white dress of exquisite details. I basked in the happy ululations and looks of admiration from Faiza's sisters as they placed a seat for me in the garden to wait for my brother.

I couldn't wait to enter our home and see myself reflected in the eyes of my sisters and aunts while we waited for the groom and his family to pick me up and take me to the wedding venue. I wondered if my father would accompany me to the wedding car or if he would leave that task to my older brother, as is customary in our family. The moment a girl leaves her family home to join her husband, accompanied by tears and joyful ululations from both her family and his, is always a memorable one.

My brother entered the garden, snatching me out of my daydreams. My husband-to-be, dressed in the finest of suits, was following him, which didn't bode well. "Why didn't you go to our house and wait for me there?" I asked Hassib. My brother held my hand and said, "Hamida . . . Father didn't want you to go back there. He asked your husband and his family to pick you up from here."

In a moment, all traces of happiness evaporated. Faiza pleaded with me, "Don't ruin your makeup," as tears streamed down my face. But what was the point of makeup now? What was left for me to celebrate when my very presence was being rejected?

I screamed at my brother and husband, and only the arrival of my cousin calmed me down. "Let's go back there now," she said. "Uncle's praying at the mosque. Quick, Auntie's waiting for us. She says Hamida has to leave from the family home like everyone else."

We got in the car, which was decorated with the most beautiful flowers, and drove back to the house. My mother rushed out with my sisters to meet me, ululating though her voice was hoarse from crying. "No need to get out of the car, my daughter," she said. "We'll follow you." Save for the noise of the car horns, it felt more like a funeral procession than a wedding.

Once in the wedding hall, I could only sit stiffly, waiting for the farce to end. The hours stretched joylessly out ahead of us. The wedding guests whispered fearfully among themselves. Security agents had made veiled women remove their headscarves before allowing them in. Even the band couldn't play until they'd produced written permission, and a security agent looked sternly over their shoulders the whole time. As for our wedding pictures, they were confiscated along with the camera after the ceremony.

Then it was finally over, and I went to my new home. The smell from my mother-in-law's incense burner suffocated me. I went into the bedroom and collapsed in tears on the chair by the dressing table. My husband came in and tried to console me, though he himself was exhausted and his health was suffering. I wanted to comfort him too but couldn't. I was unable to touch him. As he helped me out of the heavy wedding dress, I felt like every cell in my body was choking. I stiffened as I clung to my dress, just like I'd clung to my clothes when they forced me to strip in the torture room. There was a violent throbbing inside my head. I was hanging from the ceiling, naked, my body stung by their whips. God, why now? Why tonight of all nights? Must the oppressors crush everything, even the night of my dreams?

# The Night of the Police Raid

## Bouraouia Akkari

The stars had settled in the center of the sky when Amena decided to sit up, tired of tossing and turning from right to left and then back again, all the while feeling like her head was about to explode. The pain and pressure of the dark days that followed her husband's arrest were immense. It felt like her children had been orphaned, except there was no time for grieving, no condolences, and no burial for the absent parent.

What would she do now that the family's main provider was gone, and with him their only source of income? How would she pay the bills or afford medicine for her sick mother, who had to take a vast amount of pills with every meal?

What would she do when the landlord knocked on their door in the morning to demand the rent, now three months late and entering the fourth with this miserable week?

How would she face the demands of her little children, who wouldn't comprehend the words "we have no money"?

She'd resolved to work in the past, but her circumstances made it hard, and the places she applied kept turning her away. Besides, there was no one to take her place looking after the children.

She thought maybe she could work from home somehow. But she didn't have a budget to get started, and anyway how would she sell her handiwork under the watchful eyes of society and the ever-vigilant security services?

"O God, O God," she murmured in despair.

She had barely uttered the words when she heard loud knocks on the door, louder and more forceful than anyone had ever knocked at their door before. Or was it just the silence of the night that magnified the sound?

She was shaking as she rushed to the door. "Who is it? Who's there?" Her greatest fear was that her children be woken in the night by some horrible, unexpected terror. Fear seemed to have become their daily bread, the water they drank with their food, the air that they drew into their lungs. But the hammering on the door didn't leave her much time to think.

The door's wooden panels had already been kicked into submission by the time she got there. Standing in the doorway were three security agents, uniformed and holding the walkie-talkies they used to spy on the weak and vulnerable. She stood, trembling, pinned to the spot by the terror and injustice visited on her and her children for no reason, simply at the whim of the powers that be.

"Where are your children?" barked one of the agents.

She gestured weakly with one hand, not daring to speak. She wanted to say that they were sleeping, but just then she heard a cry from her son. He wanted a drink of water. But, she knew, he was also asking for there to be enough food at dinner, and even before the water and food, he was asking for a safe shelter where he could sleep in peace.

She wanted to run to her son and get him some water, but a slap from one of the policemen brought her back to her senses. To move without permission was a crime, she hadn't yet answered the question, and her two-year-old son should've known better than to ask for water in the presence of the esteemed generals. But, once she'd recovered, Amena's maternal instinct told her she had to be near her son. She asked them to let her give him a drink of water. A second, heavier, slap was all the response she got. "O God, O God," she thought. "Do these monsters know nothing of your will, and do you have no power over their brutality?"

She got up, moaning in pain, fighting back the anguish that was threatening to explode. She was wounded, and it was bleeding, but she hurried toward her son, only to find her five-year-old daughter holding him and staring back at the agents in indignation and fright, like she was asking them defiantly, "What do you want us from us at this late hour of the night? Isn't it enough, what you did to our father? Haven't you made us suffer enough already? Isn't this enough pain? Haven't we got enough problems already?" She wasn't strong enough to put it into words; childhood has its wisdom and human weakness its law. But emotions are too strong to be held captive. They can break through barriers, tear down laws.

Still in a daze, the next thing she saw was her eight-year-old walking calmly toward his siblings with a cup of water. He was completely ignoring the presence of the agents. It was like he wanted to send them a message: life was stronger. Adversity molds men like fire forges metal, and he was destined for the kind of manhood that would one day show them that injustice has an end. Real men do not break into the homes of vulnerable families in the middle of the night to terrorize children and torment mothers, breaking their pride and tainting the prime of their lives with bitterness.

By ignoring them, her son was telling them that life goes on no matter what, that he was more than ready to grow up, that he was walking steadfastly on the path to an adulthood in which he would never forget this night. Just like Amena hadn't forgotten the shock of her husband's arrest, how he was taken away for questioning and finally taken to prison after days of unimaginable torture.

Amena replayed her memories: How she'd received the news, how she had dealt with the crisis. How she had tried to keep a grip on herself and not break down in front of the children, wanting to shield their innocent souls from the bitter injustice of it.

What had their father done to deserve arrest? Was praying in a congregation a crime? Was piety a threat to national security and social harmony? Was charity toward widowed women and the poor a danger to the International Monetary Fund?

The test was harsh, and the price was high. Her husband paid it when he was dismissed from his job, and she paid it when her nerves couldn't take anymore and she had a miscarriage. While she was recovering in the hospital, still in physical pain and still struggling with her bereavement, a group of officers and soldiers burst in. These supposed defenders of the people, these guardians of national security, had come to the hospital not to arrest the incompetent medics who let patients be injected with contaminated blood, not the black marketeers who siphoned off lifesaving medicine for their own profit, not the corrupt doctors who let traffickers steal newborns from their mothers in exchange for bribes that silenced whatever was left of their conscience—no, they had come to arrest a woman whose husband had been detained, leaving her in sole charge of three children and a fourth who'd never seen the light of day, whose right to life was snatched away by the sharp blow of tyranny. As if that wasn't enough, they then dragged her away to be interrogated as she was—physically weak and sick and already prostrate before their injustice and brutality—hoping to get some information out of her that they could use to increase her husband's sentence or to find some reason to punish her too, by throwing her into the women's prison and leaving her children to fend for themselves.

She remembered how she had passed out during the interrogation, how she had collapsed time after time, sweat pouring off her brow and face. She remembered how she couldn't find the strength to speak, or even to look at their faces, despite the blows she was receiving.

When they were finally assured that she had nothing to hide and no connection with any of their false accusations, they had allowed her mother to take her home. Her mother had stayed with her until she regained some of her strength and could begin to take care of her affairs and look after the children. Only then had her mother left to go and see to her own home, having left her daughter and grandchildren enough money and food to last them until she returned to check on them. It was after her mother left that the events of that night took place.

# The Story of One Girl
# and the Hijab Ban

## Chafika Ben Hammouda

I was seventeen years old when I started reading Muslim Brotherhood books from Egypt, by the likes of Sayed Qutb and Hassan al-Banna. Zainab al-Ghazali's autobiography also really moved me. Her story inhabited my consciousness and proved to be a turning point in my thinking.

Reading those books was my way of rebelling as a teenager, which is, after all, the age of rebellion. Zainab al-Ghazali had become an example for many Arab women. She was a symbol of courage in the face of injustice. While women were marginalized all around the Arab world, al-Ghazali was waging an epic battle in the face of oppression.

I lived in a small village with a population of fewer than thirty thousand. But that tiny patch of land was plagued with police raids and arrests, with all the abuses of dignity and privacy they entailed. Since I was an only child and one of the first to wear a hijab, which at the time was limited to older women, my behavior was interpreted as a provocation to the regime. Fearing legal consequences, my family began to nag me to stop wearing it, so as to avoid trouble. I was grounded and told to wait it out until things calmed down in the village.

### That Thursday Morning in November 1991

After the morning prayer, I was gripped by an uncharacteristic fear. I had a panicked premonition that someone would barge in, find the antiregime publications hidden in our house, and realize I belonged to an unauthorized political party. Realizing I needed to do something before it was too late, I called an aunt of mine who was known for her fearlessness and begged her to hide my precious books in a field that belonged to my great-aunt.

My aunt came over immediately and took with her everything she could. As soon as she left, my fears came true: the police raided our house. The huge, intimidating men descended on us with a monstrosity that matched their appearance. Policemen were often recruited from orphanages, specially selected to match certain physical specifications; they were all tall, bulky men. They searched the house, turning it upside down, and then led me away, leaving my mother distraught.

When we arrived at the Research and Investigation Brigade headquarters in Nabeul, I found security agents waiting for me. As soon as I entered, my headscarf was pulled off with a sharp, violent tug. As I tried to recover, one of them barked at me, "What are you trying to prove with this hijab? Chastity? We can rape you while you're wearing it."

I felt suffocated, like they were physically choking me, and couldn't help but break down in tears. The questioning, which went on for hours, was full of lewd innuendo and intended mainly to harass and torment me. They then took me into a gray-walled, foul-smelling cell. I felt both grief and anger toward the state that had passed Circular 108, the law that lay like a dark cloud above us, blocking the light in our skies. It forced women to stop wearing the hijab and thwarted the hopes of those who wanted to.

Two women welcomed me in the cell and tried to console me. They smiled with a gentleness that was tainted with their own distress. One of them made space for me by her side and whispered in my ear, calmly and firmly, "Do not betray anyone or mention any names at all." The other added, "Don't confess to anything no matter how much they pressure you. Otherwise, others will be harmed."

## The Night after My Arrest

The night began to descend over the dark, foul-smelling place. It was an appropriate place for nightly torture sessions. Bats flitted between the cells. Voices rose and others fell. Sobs and cries for help echoed off the walls and rang in our heads, leaving us heartbroken and helpless. We found our only refuge and sanctuary in prayer and the Quran. We recited and cried and appealed to God, mixing up the sacred words in whatever combinations we could conjure to bring us some peace.

I couldn't sleep that night. The moans of one of my cellmates betrayed a pain that was still fresh in her wounds. The other cellmate turned and fidgeted, let out her own whimpers and sighs, and leaped up in panic at any sound of approaching footsteps.

It wasn't until twenty-seven years later that I fully understood everything about that night. I learned that one of the two detainees, who was exceptionally beautiful, had been raped in front of her husband by one of the jailers, in order to force him to confess to the charges brought against him. I also learned that she spent the rest of her life, after her release from prison, away from her family, carrying the weight of a shame that she wasn't responsible for. Her husband, too, isolated himself after his release, lived alone, and hoped for death until it finally came.

My second cellmate had also been raped multiple times. Her pride was broken, and she lost all hope in a happy life. She is still suffering to this day, still trying to heal herself and carry on.

# Hot Water

## Najet Gabsi

"Ouch! You almost burned me, Mama. Why do you like the water so hot? Leave me. I'll wash myself."

I didn't know how to respond. To myself I whispered, "Yes, I do love hot water, in winter *and* summer." Since I came out of prison after a six-month sentence, I haven't dared to use cold water. And for six years, because of an extra condition of my administrative monitoring, which wasn't even officially part of my judicial sentence, I couldn't go anywhere near the sea. During those years, I couldn't travel anywhere without permission from the police, even within the local region. Which caused me, among other things, to miss my sister's wedding. And when I did get a permit to visit the seaside, I was lying in bed with the flu.

My memory took me back to December 5, 1992, the day I stood before the judge who I later learned was nicknamed Chicken Head because of his long neck.

I thought, at first, that he would treat me fairly and acquit me of all charges, given he was a man of law and I was a law student, just like he himself had once been. It was hardly reasonable that my activities within a recognized student union organization be regarded as a crime. As someone who studied law, he was surely able to distinguish between a labor union and political activity.

I thought I would say a few words to help my case. "The police let me go on the same day I was arrested. I didn't have my ID on me. Would they have let me go if they had found illegal pamphlets on me?"

The judge sentenced me to prison based on a search report that was finalized a half hour before I appeared in court before him. My charges were belonging to an unauthorized organization and possession of illegal printed material. In vain I tried to defend myself. How could I be charged with belonging to an unauthorized organization? We were taught at university that the term "organization" referred in law to a group that has met all the requirements to be recognized. So my charge included an implicit recognition of the legality of the organization they were accusing me of illegally belonging to. Wouldn't it have made more sense to use some other term?

And anyway, how could a man of law pass a verdict without evidence? I found myself crying out that my prison sentence was unjust, but my voice found no echo inside the halls of the trial court of Sousse.

I cried and cried, feeling utterly wronged, until I was brought back to my senses by the voice of the police guard who was accompanying me out of the courtroom. He asked me to calm down; otherwise, I'd be found to be in contempt of court and my sentence would be even worse. I looked at him through eyes blurry with tears. "You still have the right to appeal," he said. I looked at him again, deeply troubled: Was everyone else so deaf to my cries that the only one left to console me was my oppressor? Had I been completely abandoned?

In the prison van, there were two other women, one of them a classmate of mine. The vehicle headed for the civilian prison in the old city of Sousse. I had come to this beautiful coastal city to make my father's dream come true: to study to be a lawyer and help him escape the clutches of poverty.

Once at the prison, I calmed down and tried to find some reserves of patience inside me. What's done is done, I thought.

We stood before the prison governor, a handsome, mild-mannered man. Or so it seemed to me. He summoned his deputy, whose name was Ghazal but who looked nothing like a gazelle. I whispered to my classmate, "Doesn't look much like a *ghazal* to me." He saw me chuckle and seemed to have read my mind. "Funny, is it?" he bellowed and reached his hand to slap me. If I hadn't darted quickly out of the way, the force of his heavy palm on my face would have probably thrown me to the ground.

Ghazal led us to the lockers where prisoners deposited their valuables. We handed over the little money and jewelry we had before being led down a narrow passage to an old wooden door that opened onto the yard where recreation time was spent. I later learned that people called it "l'aréa." It didn't occur to me then that this space would become my refuge of hope throughout my sentence, where I would spend most of my days contemplating the changes in the weather.

The guard opened another wooden door, made up of two panels, and delivered us to our fate. He deposited us amid a crowd of female inmates, with whom I thought I had nothing in common. I was wrong. Later I even ended up defending one of the prisoners who was there on criminal charges, a woman who used to work in a brothel in Kairouan.

I was surrounded by more than twenty women. Looking around, I suddenly found myself face-to-face with my friend Sa'ida, a beautiful, cheerful engineer from Nabeul. She greeted me with a hearty laugh, "Najet!"

"Sa'ida!"

"Welcome to our humble abode! Come in—make yourself at home. Prison is for the brave."

It did me good to hear her laugh. How did she manage to stay so calm? Having Sa'ida there brought me the comfort I was in desperate need of.

She began to introduce me to some of the inmates, who seemed to me like nice women. I found a spot near her that was already occupied by another inmate, and we shared it. I began to understand what it meant to share, in every aspect of life: sleeping space, food, hope, pain.

I gathered myself together, performed my ablutions, and began to look for a place to pray. One of the inmates told me, "Come pray over here." She looked to her friend and added, "This one seems nicer." Her friend replied, "The other one had such intimidating eyes, she could've been a judge!" They were talking about my classmate, who was lucky enough to go back to her studies after she got out of prison and is now qualified as a lawyer.

My mom always used to say a particular prayer for me: "May God bless you with the kindness of strangers and the love of his Prophet." The welcoming words of the two women gave me some reassurance that her prayer was being answered.

Time passed slowly in prison. The days dragged and their monotony was suffocating, with nothing on the horizon to promise any kind of change.

About once every two weeks we would leave the wing for our long-awaited communal showers. It was miserable to spend all that time without the feel of water on your skin, especially if you were accustomed to showering on a daily basis. There was hot water in the showers, but we were given hardly any time. So, often, we had to rinse ourselves with cold water in the lavatory on the wing. You could hear the gasp from the other side of the ward when the cold water hit someone's skin, especially in winter. We'd suffer from colds for days afterward, and we never had access to medication. The skin on my upper lip became so cracked from the recurring colds, I have scars there to this day.

When I showered on the wing, I would use a pot that was provided by the prison administration for our "little prisoner," the infant child of one of the inmates. She was also given a little bit of hot water to wash him each morning. The only thing that could distract me from the agony of cold water was the adorable giggle of baby 'Adel when I brought the pot back to his mother, as if he knew that both pot and hot water were valuable currency in that place.

"That, sweetheart," I wanted to tell my daughter, "is why I can't stand cold water."

# Let Us Celebrate

## Aouatef Mezghani

Every Eid, I announce to myself and others that I don't like Eid. Every Eid, I wipe away my tears with a stubborn smile and try to celebrate. Every Eid, I murmur, "Enough tears. Enough sorrow. I will try to forget." But, every year, I realize I have forgotten to forget.

The Eid chants that fill the air and the festive delight that's everywhere you look—in the streets, on shop fronts, on the faces of children, in the voices of peddlers singing the praises of their goods, in the car horns pleading for passage through the joyful madness of it all—it's all there, like the soundtrack of a favorite movie. The moment I hear it, my mind conjures up the details of the scene, of everything I thought I had left behind but that had stubbornly stayed with me. Ever since that time, the memory has constantly resided in the background of my life, like a film playing on repeat, a soundtrack that never fades. But as long as the story of that Eid has not been told, it will remain trapped under layers of pain and sorrow. It's a story that has remained locked inside me all this time. Its details live behind my eyes and fill them with tears that refuse to flow. That's why I have decided to write: twenty-five Eids, and countless memories.

### Prison

I didn't know how long the night of June 9, 1992, planned to last. The anticipation was dreadful. Fear—though not without a tiny dose of naive hope mixed in—took over every cell in my body and throbbed loudly in my head. From time to time I let out a sigh to release some of what was burning within me, but it only made me feel more suffocated. My lungs constricted with every jab of pain. I would look around me and find every-one lost in a separate world. So many worlds were gathered in that small dark room, making its air heavy. When we made eye contact, our smiles were weak and confused, forced upon us by an illusory obligation to try to give each other some warmth. I looked away, in a desperate attempt to gather what was left of my courage. With accelerating breath, I looked out of the opening above my head. I registered the sound of cars speeding past on the road adjacent to the prison. I glimpsed a few stars sparkling like frozen tears refusing to flow. Through loudspeakers, the mosques near the prison announced to the kingdom of their Creator the arrival of Eid, then recited some of the Quran.

In my mind's eye, I could see the many gifts of Eid: the chants, the joy on children's faces, the calls of street vendors, the whistles of traffic police trying in vain to impose some discipline and get people to pay some atten-tion to traffic laws, the loud cries of the crowded street, the faces hopeful for a share of the feast, the outstretched palms urging passersby to share a little of what was in their generous pockets, and maybe some of the Eid spirit would trickle down to their children too.

"What if the worst happens and after the trial we find ourselves back in this hole? What if, at the end of the day, we're destined to lose?" one of the detainees wondered aloud.

Another replied in a choked voice, "We won't make it. No, no—we will make it. We must."

A third woman, who kept a calm facade throughout our ordeal, said in a bright, encouraging voice, "Go easy on yourselves—and on the rest of us, too! God willing, everything will turn out fine."

Their words made my head spin. They darted from their lips straight to my ears, agitated, full of pain, striking me like a hammer and almost knocking me over. I was panicking. I couldn't think any of the predictions through, even though I knew full well that one or another of them would become a reality in a matter of hours.

I awoke from the inferno of the night to the sting of cold water pour-ing out of the tap over my head, the brush pressing through my soaking hair, and the involuntary gasps that hurt my chest. I tried to convince my-self that the temperature of the water was bearable. I closed my eyes and held my breath and let it cool the feverish clamor of my thoughts. Finally, in response to reminders from my fellow inmates to hurry up because others were waiting in line for the shower, looking forward to their dose of freezing water, I turned off the tap.

## The Road to Court

Rays of light, stacked in one corner of the room, announced the arrival of morning. One day to go until Eid al-Adha. I couldn't tell if it felt too late or too soon. I'd lost all sense of time in that suffocating cell with its high small windows, blocked with rusted iron bars and a glass pane that was firmly shut, only letting through a pallid semblance of sunshine.

Things moved fast. The early hours of the morning raced by, hurrying toward the time of the trial. The cell was filled with a din of voices, both tearful and cheerful, oscillating between optimism and despair. The tension played havoc with our nerves and refracted our attention. The questions tormented us. I glanced around at my companions and saw a silent sorrow mixed with a timid, concealed hope. "Let the day pass in peace," said one of them.

One of the prison guards came to take us to court. I noticed that her smile was more blasé, more sardonic than usual; there was something gloating about her features. Her presence made us more boisterous and disorderly. Unthinkingly, I clenched my hand into a fist. I wanted to punch her, to push her away. I stared at the ceiling more purposefully in an attempt to suppress my feelings and recited some verses from the Holy Quran to calm myself and transcend her provocations. She approached, her arms crossed over her chest, looked around the room, and let her gaze linger on our troubled faces, relishing the torment she evoked in us and deliberately stubbing out the expressions of hope she found on the faces of some. Then she came closer and said in an exaggeratedly loud voice, "You're just going out for a little day trip, and then you're coming back. You'll spend your Eid here with us."

There are times when all you can do is swallow the bitterness of the moment in silence and hold on to whatever strength you can summon. I had to find the resilience to face the mocking looks of the prison guards, which made light of our suffering and dismissed our pain. The door banged shut behind us. They led us through a narrow, moldy, stuffy passage. I was shivering as if whipped by a cold winter breeze, even though it was a hot day. A chill passed from my toes to the top of my head. I fixed my gaze on the exit door, as if some salvation might lie there. I was looking for anything that would bring comfort to my eyes and my heart, anything to carry us closer to freedom, closer to our loved ones.

It was hard to achieve while we sat in a prison van made like an iron box with no openings but a few vents, so small as if deliberately meant to remind the van's passengers of how confined they were in there, compared to the outside world. I brought my nose closer to one of the vents that seemed to me to be a little wider than the others and took in a deep breath. I felt the air slip in, almost playfully, filling my lungs. For a moment, the surprising sensation of air refreshed me—it was almost as if I could feel the individual molecules enter my lungs, excited and uncertain, like my mood.

Through these small vents, I could just see the signs of Eid outside: the colors and festive decorations everywhere, street vendors, children carrying colorful balloons—everyone and everything seemed to fill the roads, the shops, the streetlights, with the spirit of the feast. The only exception was the few people waiting for the prison van, with eyes worn from weeping and uncertain looks as they frantically tried to locate a loved one, a wife or a daughter—only they were not touched by Eid's joyful colors.

They brought us out of the van and into the courtroom quickly so no one would get a chance to see us. I immediately felt how cramped and cold the place was. The citadels where "justice is served," as the phrase went, were crushing me underfoot. A heavy silence hung over my heart. I threw my gaze to the other end of the hall, searching among the silently screaming faces for my father, my husband, someone carrying one of my children—Marwa, Omar, or the little one, Alaa—and for my mother, especially for my mother . . . Oh, how I missed her, how the heavy days dragged without her!

I couldn't make out any of them. The faces were all the same, all contemplating the same pain.

I turn to glance around the place again when someone yelled at me, "Face forward! You're not allowed to turn around!"

I almost yelled back, "When have you ever allowed us to look forward?"

## The Trial

The facts of the case: affiliation to and retention of an unlicensed organization, holding meetings, providing premises for meetings, distributing antigovernment publications, graffiti, fund-raising.

Courtroom: a grim and imposing hall, a table like a massive barrier, the gavel of justice waiting to fall hard on the table.

Presiding judges: black suits, dark faces.

The accused: mothers, wives, daughters, sisters.

Attendance: parents, spouses and children, brothers and sisters, in agony for their loved ones.

A group of lawyers, frustrated and angry, in the middle of the courtroom.

The trial: a tragicomedy, the paperwork stating the verdicts already prepared, the conviction indisputable, and the confessions signed and sealed.

It was a short trial, a mockery of our suffering. The charges were brought against us, and "justice" was swiftly served.

We stood there helpless, sapped of any strength or speech, filled with emotion while our lives were dying inside us. We waited. We waited where waiting was futile and survival impossible. We stood there, vulnerable and exposed in our homeland, the whips of justice striking our souls before our bodies. We stood there, with no cause, no defeat, no heroism, just a void overflowing with pain. The judges left us there, our souls broken and scattered, and exited the hall accompanied by an uproar from the gallery, a noise like the beating of drums on our heads. If you're ever asked about the judiciary in my country, tell them it's the scales of justice inverted and deformed, an arena of sophisticated brutality, a greenhouse of withering rights, a mill that grinds the disadvantaged classes to the bone.

I was overcome by weakness once more, but this time I tried to force a smile. Who knew? Maybe my father or mother would see me, and my smile would reassure them a little. I saw the row of those there to witness justice being done in my country, to witness our tragic fall, and that was the last straw. I couldn't control myself any longer. I looked around again, in the hope that my eyes would chance upon one of my loved ones. A tremor went through me, and, despite my best efforts, my tears started falling hot on my cheeks. I smiled through my tears and looked around one last time before the guards started dragging us away for the return journey to prison. I was wishing so hard for a glimpse of my mother, wanting to fill my senses with her presence. Only her embrace would have been capable of giving me strength. Her absence broke me, exposing how weak and lost I was without her.

Among the craned necks and searching eyes, I made out my father. His face was dark with fury. I didn't know if it was because of the trial or if he was angry with me. I couldn't think straight. All I knew was that I missed him very much. No! Of course he wasn't angry with me. He was choking and dying inside at the sight of me in this state. How could he not be, when his own daughter was being locked away before his eyes and he knew he could do nothing to stop it? Maybe his sense of helplessness was making him suffer. Maybe . . . I looked to him, pleading for his approval, his love, his prayers, and his patience. I wanted to ask him to take good care of my children, but was immediately ashamed of the thought because I knew that both he and my mother were more attentive to my children's needs than I could ever be. I embraced him with my eyes. That was when he welled up, his tears pouring down his cheeks. I had never seen my father cry before. I saw how he tried to hold back the tears, gritting his teeth in an attempt to resist them, closing his eyes as if he were imploring them to hold off, and then how he suddenly let go. At the same moment, I felt a powerful shove from someone behind me that propelled me through the courtroom entrance toward the prison van.

Inside me was a chess board where white and black alternated disconcertingly. My prison comrades and I were like lost, helpless pawns, shoved around by the hands playing the game. We struggled in vain to fix ourselves on a white patch, but the black pulled at us and the hands kept throwing us toward it.

### The Road to Prison

The road took me and the others back to the prison cell. My sentence was several months of prison and an unquantifiable mass of grief and pain.

My tears continued to flow soundlessly. I cried as if the tears were washing away all my sins. But it was still only half the crying I really felt like. The other half I forced myself to swallow. I hated to be weak. I still hoped that my determination could save me. My friend whispered my name, and I looked up at her. "Don't cry. Everything happens by the will of God," she said in a soft whisper full of tenderness and then hugged me. I surrendered to the warmth of her gesture and felt momentarily better. Maybe those moments were enough to grant each of us a place in the other's memory for good. I needed that hug to calm my frantic heart, needed to feel the rhythm of her breathing between my ribs and let it calm my own. When I spoke, it was without filter. "Oh God, I feel like my heart is burning." I couldn't believe that my children wouldn't be in my arms on the eve of Eid and that I was back in this tiny iron box.

When they decided to force us back to that cell, did they know they were tying the shackles of injustice around my wrists? Left with the shackles and their blood-soaked mark on my wrists, could I smile? There was no pain greater than this pain, so I might as well smile.

On the way back, I didn't look out of the van. I wanted to banish Eid from my thoughts and imagine that it had skipped this year out of respect for our tears and the tears of our children and parents. I was drowning in my grief and frustration, crushed under the heavy soles of injustice. The noise around me began to subside. I turned to find that we were already at the big prison door, the monster that opened with a screech that pierced my heart every time. I looked at my friend, who sat beside me with half a smile, to find the traces of tears still covering her face. I pulled her hand and clasped it lightly in mine to give her some of the warmth I had. I wanted to recharge her as she had done with me, give her some of the positive energy that we need to see us through the long, wretched hours ahead.

### The Day of the Visit

Sleep was unattainable that night. I stared at the ceiling and let my eyes roam its shabby grayness, the only emptiness in a place that was crowded with exhausted bodies. I fixed my eyes on the yellow lighting, which held a night watch over our nightmares. I could make out the threads of a spider that must have lost its way, for why else would it make its home here? Gradually, numbness crept in and lulled me to sleep.

The rays of the sun crept out stealthily from behind the clouds to embrace the gray sky. Dawn rose slowly. The sun was surrounded by threads of darkness, a reflection of my having lived through the previous night. I had reached the height of exhaustion after many hours of insomnia before the sound of chanting hit my ears: It was Eid al-Adha! In this loathsome place where everything was different—pain wasn't like ordinary pain, fear wasn't like ordinary fear, absence wasn't like absence, or longing like longing—Eid was nothing like Eid. Everything here was different.

We learned that we would be receiving visits from our families. The guards came to us with their insults, roaring like summer storms, and ordered us to get ready for the visits. They checked our faces with eyes full of glee, keen to make us presentable in a way that would reflect well on their dedication to their jobs. They pulled the cover off a woman's head, ordered another to take off her socks, adjusted and readjusted our hair. "The custom of Eid is to show a portion of the hair," they said.

We stood in a row, heads lowered, ashamed of what we were made to show of our bodies. The door was opened, letting in the pale light from the narrow passage. At the other end of it, by a battered wall, we were pushed into the visiting hall. The passageway that took us to our loved ones made me feel suffocated—it was cold and bleak and deeply lonely. Despite the short distance, it took forever to get through it. I wanted to get there quicker.

Questions crowded in my head.

Who had come? Marwa, Omar, or Alaa? Or all of them? Were they there with my mother, with my father, or was my husband the one who brought them? Would I be allowed to hug them, kiss them, smell them? Had Eid reached them with its light and colors? What colors would they be wearing? Would they be in Eid clothes? Who had chosen their clothes for them? Who had bathed and clothed and perfumed them? How was my mother? How was she handling the absence of her daughter, the mother of her grandchildren?

In the visit hall, each prisoner took her place where her family was. We were separated from our loved ones by two wire-mesh barriers, one erected in front of us, the other in front of our families. The two sides were two meters apart, and in the space between the two barriers, a group of guards paced up and down. I searched the faces of my visitors. So much longing and pain. My heart felt like it was about to stop. I pushed my fingers through the holes in the wire, as if that way I could reach the soft cheek of one of my children.

"Mama! Milk!" my tiny son babbled at me. Alaa was still breast-feeding when I was arrested. He was too young, and he hadn't yet gotten over his abrupt weaning, so as soon as he saw me, he asked for his milk. He pointed his small hands at me and continued to cry. Marwa stood on her tiptoes and stretched out her hand to show me the henna that her auntie had drawn for her. It was the closest we got to a hug. I noticed that Omar's face was red. I didn't know if he'd gotten sunburned while waiting to come in for the visit or if he was perhaps sick. I wished I could feel his forehead and put my lips to his cheeks, kiss him, and smell his scent. I looked from my children to my parents to my husband. We were all staring at each other's faces with tearful eyes, for why wouldn't we cry when our wounded souls were silenced? Their tears were as soundless as their silent souls.

In that rust-suffused grayness that surrounded us, I glimpsed my mother: her eyes were unfocused, staring at the emptiness behind me, her face blank but for a silent stream of tears down her cheeks. A numbness overtook me, a paralysis even. Do you know that feeling of paralysis? Not quite an inability to move, no. The paralysis of that day was the worst of all, the failure of my feet to carry me to them, to their embrace, the failure of my fingers to touch theirs.

In the presence of my loved ones—only a few steps away but unable to breathe in their smell, touch their faces, hold their hands—I went completely quiet on the inside, mute even. I just tried to memorize their features, even the colors of their clothes, so I could carry that back to my cell, hold it tight, and fall asleep. Oh God, I wasn't in a position then to ask for justice, but what I asked for in that moment was just a lesser degree of injustice and a slightly higher degree of humanity. That's all I asked for. Not for me, but for them.

Around us there were screaming and crying, the greetings of Eid along with the sounds of kisses in the air. A mélange of pain and joy that was interrupted by the bellows of the jailers announcing the end of the visit. When the prison guard led me away from my family, the cry of my son lingered, "We want to stay with you, Mama!" My other children seemed bewildered. Their incessant weeping rang in my head. But the worst was my father's silence.

I was awoken from my quasi coma by a torrent of insults from one of the guards. "Do you think you're Aziza Othmana or Majida Boulila, you worthless fucking whor—"

I wasn't paying attention to her at first. My grief was greater than her and her insults, but then I sprang up like I was touched by madness. I suddenly wanted to jump on her, tear at her with my teeth, like she tore away my humanity and my motherhood. "Enough! Enough!" I found myself screaming, "What more do you want? I hope God will punish you in your children!"

The room's lights came on, signaling another sad, bleak evening. I realized that Eid would be gone before we'd had a chance to gain anything from it but pain. I looked around me, my senses suddenly alert. With the back of my hand, I wiped away the tears that had escaped my eyes. I started to find the remnants of my lost voice, to return to my resilience.

I said, "Is this not a day of Eid?" Everyone gave me puzzled looks, so I added, "Well, it's tit for tat, and they started it. They wanted to make us miserable today, so let us take our revenge by celebrating the holy feast. There will be future Eids to make up for this one, but perhaps we were brought together to experience a different kind of Eid. The memory of this Eid will remain a witness to everything we've been through, but let us invest ourselves in forgetting for some hours, in spite of those who stand gloating over our misfortune. Let's rejoice in an Eid unlike all the others. Isn't Eid a gift from God? God's gifts should not be refused. The way to honor his gifts is to receive them properly, and the purpose of Eid is to provide an opportunity for hope to flow into hearts beset by despair."

In the space of a few moments, the room exploded with Eid celebrations.

# Part Three
# Testimony
## Tunisia in Color

# On the Margins of the Path

## Mounira Ben Kaddour Toumi

What frightens me more than anything is not change per se, because change itself is a natural thing. "Time changes the perception of things," as Einstein might have once said. What frightens me is how fast change can happen.

For me personally, through the different stages of my life, I have discovered unexpected aspects not only in myself, but in my interactions with others and with my environment.

I wasn't interested in such things at the time of the Tunisian revolution. I was busy getting ready for my son's marriage in late December: preparing and furnishing the newlyweds' home and planning the wedding and other events around it. Then immediately after the wedding, I flew to Italy with my sister to visit my sick aunt, who was like a second mother to me. She was afraid of dying all alone and had been asking us to visit for a while. She was my godmother and had carried me with her husband during my baptism, and I had lived with her for a while when she was still in Tunisia.

I stayed with my aunt until her passing and burial and then returned to Tunisia a day or two before President Ben Ali's escape. Once back home, I followed the news of the revolution sporadically. I was preoccupied with my husband's illness, which we had discovered days before our son's wedding. My mind was busy with questions. Do we tell him the truth about his illness? Should we tell him that it had gotten to the point where it wouldn't get better and that there was no treatment left to try? Should we tell him what the doctor had told me, that he had only six months to live?

I deliberated over and over with the doctor, who advised me not to tell him the truth, because it could destroy his morale rather than help him and that the despondency resulting from that knowledge might trigger a rapid psychosomatic deterioration. It's sometimes more important to give a patient hope than to keep them well informed, and it may allow them a psychological tranquillity that will positively affect their physical health. Or, as the tenth-century physician Al-Razi said, "The status of the body's disposition is dependent on the manners of the spirit."

For all those reasons, I found myself on the margins of the revolution. While I was following the news on television, including all the commentary and analysis from inside and outside Tunisia, and discussing everything with my husband, I did so as a witness, not as an active participant. Perhaps, also, I just couldn't imagine that Tunisians, having lived quietly for half a century with an unjust dictatorship that held us all under heavy surveillance in an open-air prison, would actually one day rise up.

I didn't imagine that Tunisians, who had been silent in the face of injustice and tyranny all those years, enduring oppression and humiliation, these long-suffering people who seemed content with so little, would actually see this revolution through to its end. But they surprised me as they surprised the whole world. For the first time I had a sense of belonging and felt real pride to be part of this people and this country. I realized that silence in the face of oppression and injustice was not cowardice but extreme tolerance and forgiveness and that being content with little was a sign not of weakness but of love for the homeland.

The wider revolution was the beginning of another revolution within myself and in my relationship with the homeland and everything in it.

For many years I had lived on the margins of Tunisian society. The daughter of an Italian single mother, I grew up in a Western Christian environment. Even when the rest of my Italian family left Tunisia, most of my mother's friends were Italian and Western women married to Tunisians. The few Tunisian connections we had included my father's family, who had never been happy about his divorce from my mother and remained on friendly, loving terms with her.

I went to public schools, but hardly made any friends, with the exception of two classmates who were—and still remain—exceptionally free of prejudices and accepting of "the other." Their families had welcomed me with open arms, without interrogating me about my background and roots.

I became aware of standing out after a particularly hurtful encounter with a classmate's mother at the age of twelve. We had the beginnings of a friendship when one day my classmate invited me over to her house, which was next to the school. When I got there, her mother questioned me about my name, my father's name, my mother's name, my father's job, my ancestors, my grandparents, my links to this and that. I answered her innocently, but noticed how her face and tone changed and knew that somehow my answers did not satisfy her.

When I saw my supposed-friend-in-the-making the next day, she told me that her mother had vetoed our friendship on the basis that we were not of the same milieu and background, or, in her mother's humiliating words, "On ne mélange pas les serviettes et les torchons."[1] We went through our school years without interacting much. Years later, I once heard her say, in a conversation about boys, "I'm only interested in king prawns. Small fish aren't even worth a glance."

Thinking about the world today, it looks like the *serviettes* have been left behind, buried at the back of the cupboard and rarely used anymore, while the *torchons*—which is just French for "dishcloths"—remain indispensable. Plus, prawns aren't so good for your health, but cheap fishlike sardines are full of nutrients.

During my youth, I hung out at expats' clubs. Then I went into the tourism industry and worked in most of its sectors, from a travel agency to a tourist development company to hotels. Throughout my career, I was in constant contact with foreigners and traveled extensively to market our top product—that is, Tunisia itself.

In the late 1980s, a new phenomenon emerged in our society, namely, religiosity. Many Tunisians rejected it, and I was one of them. At the time, I was a member of an international charitable organization. During one of our monthly meetings, the women present discussed this phenomenon.

1. "We don't mix towels and rags."

We also touched on the Islamic movement, which was beginning to be active politically, a fact that worried us, especially the possibility that success in parliamentary elections (the movement's members stood as "independents") would open the door to legitimate political involvement and eventually put Islamists in decision-making positions. We wondered what we'd do if the Islamists succeeded in their political objectives and got to a point where they could change the laws of the country and perhaps go on to make us all wear the hijab, as had happened in Iran.

One of those present said she'd rather remain housebound for the rest of her life than wear a headscarf. Another said she would prefer to shave her head. My response was that I would never wear a headscarf or do anything under pressure, that I would continue to go out as I was, at whatever price, and that my short dress and my long hair blowing in the wind would be a form of resistance.

But none of that happened. The Islamists never became a legitimate part of political life. On the contrary, a harsh campaign was waged against its members and supporters.

My antihijab stance aside, I didn't pay any attention to what happened to opponents of the regime, whatever their ideological and political affiliation. Like many in the country, I knew very little, and what I did know was hearsay. I wasn't personally invested in what I heard, and because most of it was so harrowing, it seemed like it must be fabricated or exaggerated.

The shock came when I joined a women's organization after the revolution. It was one of the first to bring to light some of the gross human rights violations of the past regime in general, since adopting the cause of female political prisoners in January 2012, the violation of women's rights in particular. We issued several calls asking former women prisoners to come forward with their stories.

As I listened to the testimonies, I discovered that I was indeed living on the margins of Tunisian society and not within it. I used to have a running joke with a colleague in the hotel where I worked. Whenever I didn't understand something that was happening outside the hotel, he would tell me, "In here, we're in the Tourist Republic. Out there it's the Republic of Tunisia."

I was moved and shocked to find out about the violations. The stories I heard made a painful impression on me and left me with a bitterness that will stay with me for the rest of my days. I had never thought that a human being, with a thinking mind and a feeling heart, was capable of inflicting that kind of torture on another human being. The irony is that the perpetrators of those horrors were the so-called security services. What kind of security could that be?

Listening to the testimony of a victim-survivor about what was done to her, I would struggle to believe the excess of brutality, which ranged from beatings, insults, and humiliations to stripping women naked, tying them up and hanging them like chickens, forcing them to sit on bottles, and other preposterous forms of torture that were in fact completely routine. I felt the women's pain and cried with them. I wanted to throw myself on the ground to kiss their feet and ask them to forgive me, because I, like the majority of Tunisians, had never imagined the magnitude of the abuses. If I had heard about them, I would have said little or nothing at all. I would have blamed the victims, saying, "They must be guilty of something. And those claims are obviously exaggerated." But mostly, I just kept my head in the sand. Our silence was a form of support for a tyrannical, corrupt regime. Our silence allowed the regime to become more brutal, repressive, and inhumane.

In an attempt to absolve myself, I often asked at the end of a testimony, "What had you done to get arrested?" hoping I would hear a confession to a crime so serious that it would partially warrant such awful punishment. But I knew perfectly well that however great the crime, there was no justification for the crimes of the regime. What could possibly justify torturing a young woman because she taught children the Quran? What could possibly legitimize causing her to miscarry, while she begged and pleaded and told her torturer she was pregnant, only for him to continue to beat her on the stomach, saying, "Well, then, I'll get rid of this little traitor for you"? And what could explain the arrest of another woman, who was left wondering, "Can anyone tell me why I was arrested and tortured? I have no political or ideological affiliation, and I didn't even wear a headscarf!"? All this one had done was advise her roommates at the student dorm to stay chaste. Being from a conservative background, she would see them hanging out with boys and getting into relationships, so she'd tell them the only story she knew from the Quran, the story of the prophet Yusuf and his chastity. Was that a crime? And did that "crime" deserve the kinds of torture she was subjected to, like being made to sit naked on a glass bottle, swaying back and forth because it was impossible to keep her balance, until it broke under her and cut her feet? What about the two girls who were raped at the ages of nine and eleven because their mother refused to give up the hijab and cursed Ben Ali? Or the woman who was hung by the wrists alongside her husband, after the customary tearing and stripping of clothes? They were told while they were being whipped, "This is our wedding present to you. This is our present to celebrate your honeymoon." Their crime? A month earlier they had gotten married without seeking permission from the security services. Or the man who tearfully begged his mother, "Forgive me, Mother! Forgive me for not being able to defend you when they arrested you. Or when they tortured you. Or when they imprisoned you"? He was eleven years old when his mother was arrested in front of him.

### The Day I Started Wearing the Hijab

It was a weekend, and I went out to do the weekly shopping. That was the only aspect of normality about that day. That day was the dividing line between two different states, which cut to the core of who I was. The first problem I faced was what to wear. I didn't have any clothes that suited my new situation other than the *jilbab* I wore for praying. The previous day, I had bought two headscarves to cover my hair but hadn't given much thought to the rest. I thought that since I'd started to pray, I'd been wearing longer dresses and skirts anyway and more trousers. I just put on what I found and went out, my heart beating so hard it felt like it was leaving my chest, so nervous I thought my breathing would stop. I gave myself a pep talk. "What's wrong with you? It's just clothes! What are you so nervous about? Take it easy. Haven't we been thinking this over for a while now? Are we not doing this with awareness and conviction? Is all of this fear? But fear of what? Fear of whom? What do we have to fear? We haven't done anything wrong. Have we broken any laws? Heck, we haven't done anyone any harm, nor do we intend to. We're not committing a crime, okay? So why the fear then? Also, remember there's no fear but the fear of God Almighty, and whatever happens, it will be for the best."

My decision to wear the hijab was the result of a gradual intellectual and spiritual journey that came from within me, from my own choices, with no coercion or even encouragement from anyone else. In my circles, whether familial, professional, or social, women did not cover their heads. Few even prayed. So my religious journey was a personal one. For years before I started wearing a headscarf, I had searched in vain for someone to teach me more about my religion. I took to the books that were available in bookstores, but they didn't satisfy me. Then I joined a Sufi group that was allowed to be active at the time, provided that the women followers (the *fakirs*) (in general, the term is used for both males and females, though writing it in Arabic you can differentiate, *faqir* for males and *faqirat* for females, so I think *faqirat* is a better translation) were not wearing a hijab when they either entered or left the prayer hall (the one exception being the "traditional Tunisian" kerchief) and that all members left a copy of their IDs at the precinct located next to the prayer hall.

Sufism had a great impact on me, especially in terms of self-improvement, renouncing materialism, and developing the experiential spirituality that elevates one above worldly desires. Those were all things I admired and loved, but I did not learn much about the fundamentals of religion. And I remained thirsty for that knowledge. That thirst was like a fire raging in my heart. But there was nowhere in Tunisia where I could openly seek that religious education.

Wearing the hijab wasn't itself easy or without negative consequences. The ruling party fought it in myriad ways, which ranged from intimidation to threats, from verbal to physical violence and a variety of torture methods that were the speciality of the authorities. That's why it surprises me when I hear those opposed to the hijab say that women wear it only under pressure from their father, brother, or husband! Do they say that out of experience, or is it mere rhetoric to justify their opposition to it? You will rarely find a Tunisian woman who does anything against her will, especially in the cities. Besides, for someone to choose this thorny path, it must be her choice and a reflection of her own will, given the reactions and consequences she knows she would have to face.

When I started wearing the hijab, it came as a surprise to my family, including my husband and children. Reactions ranged from surprise to ridicule and wavered between acceptance and rejection. I explained my motivations, and most understood my point of view but still worried about the harassment I might face. There was one who rejected my choice so completely, she declared an ongoing war that has lasted even after the revolution—whether out of concern for me or for herself or both, I will probably never know!

Some did not understand my point of view but respected it and said, "This is your personal freedom. If you are convinced, we respect your choice. It doesn't matter if we understand it or not." This was in particular the position of a close friend of mine. Isn't that what makes our diversity such a rainbow? Isn't it what makes it the most glorious painting in the sky, after the storm has subsided? No matter what our colors, our rights remain the same.

Appendix A

Appendix B

Contributors

# Circular 108

### Excerpt from a Legal Paper on Circular 108
### Prepared by Justice Anwar Munsir

The de facto hijab ban in Tunisia came into force in 1981 when then-president Habib Bourguiba issued Circular 108 banning female students, teachers, and public sector employees from wearing "sectarian dress" in state institutions such as schools, universities, hospitals, and government facilities. This ban was renewed with Circular 102 in 1986 and then again in 2001 by Zine El Abidine Ben Ali, with Circular 35.

The circular permitted the violation of the rights of those wearing the hijab on the grounds that the hijab constituted sectarian dress. Many women were deprived of the right to take up public service employment, and many others were suspended or dismissed for their choice of dress, thus deprived of their constitutionally secured right to work. Many young women were also deprived of their constitutional right to education by the provisions of the circular.

It is also worth noting that the circular constituted a flagrant affront to the principle of separation of powers, since rights and freedoms could only, according to the constitution, be restricted by legislation. Such legislation would have had to clearly mandate the executive (including ministers), which exercised regulatory powers, to take the necessary measures to implement any such restriction. The constitution also specified that any restriction of a right or freedom be justified by reference to a threat to the rights of others, public order, national defense, economic development, or social progress. It is therefore clear that this attempt to

First presented as "Circular 108 from the Perspective of Transitional Justice," at a roundtable organized by Association Femmes de Tunisie and held at Golden Tulip El Mechtel Hotel on Saturday, May 9, 2015.

limit freedom of dress—and thereby, implicitly, freedom of conscience also—was never lawful. It also exceeded the scope of a circular—in theory a document issued internally to provide an interpretation of previous legislative and precedent-establishing texts for the purpose of assisting public administration employees in their correct application. It is patently clear that Circular 108 diverged from this intended aim, which was to explain and simplify previously enacted legal stipulations, by making binding general stipulations that directly affected the legal status of the addressee. On this basis, a number of cases were heard before the Administrative Tribunal, not to strike down the circular but to overturn decisions made on the basis of the circular. Finally, around 2006, the court overturned a number of these decisions, on the grounds that it was not demonstrated that the plaintiffs were wearing sectarian dress and that the public administration was unable to disprove their claims that they were following the traditional Tunisian practice of wearing a *taqrita*.[1]

As concerns the implementation of these rulings, there are no recorded legal cases suggesting refusal of implementation. In a departure from the court's previous approach, which was to examine the facts of the case alone, in December 2006 a preliminary ruling on the matter was issued, in which the court overturned a dismissal from employment on the grounds of the unlawfulness of the circular itself and a consequent lack of jurisdiction. It considered "that Circular 108 grants the public administration unlimited discretionary power in its application, producing a threat to basic freedoms including freedom of conscience, which is constitutionally guaranteed; and that it is used as a means to constrain individual rights and freedoms."

### Administrative Monitoring[2]

Administrative monitoring—understood as a form of state surveillance and control—was used at various points throughout Tunisian history to suppress dissent

---

1. The *taqrita*, derived from a verb meaning "to tie tightly," is a square kerchief of any color that is folded into a triangle and used to hold back the hair without covering it entirely (usually the bangs or front section of the head remain visible). It is often said to be Amazigh in origin. The term *taqrita* refers to this style of head covering rather than the practice of covering itself.

2. Extracts from "Citizens under Siege: Administrative Monitoring in Tunisia," a report from the International Association for the Support of Political Prisoners, Tunis, Mar. 2010.

and maintain control over its citizens. This included members of the national-ist movement as punishment for their involvement in the struggle for national liberation and against members of the Youssefist movement that disagreed with Bourguiba over the internal autonomy agreement with France. Administrative monitoring was also directed at many leftists, nationalists, and Islamists in the period until 1987, when Bourguiba was removed from power. But Islamists and leftists were again subjected to these measures following the political trials of the 1990s, as were thousands of young Tunisians tried under the law of December 10, 2003 (the so-called Anti-Terrorism Act), until the end of 2010.

Administrative monitoring in Tunisia included the following measures:

- A requirement for the released political prisoner to regularly register at-tendance at a security precinct, generally multiple times per day or week, a trip that often included excessively long wait times.
- Denial of the right to work and the right to free movement. A released political prisoner was required to remain at the address specified in the administrative monitoring order and was not allowed to leave their area of residence (village, municipality, or city) or move houses without prior permission from the authorities responsible for implementing the admin-istrative monitoring order. Such permission was usually difficult to obtain and entailed prolonged negotiations and delays.
- Administrative monitoring could last for a period of one to five years when mandated by the courts, but could be extended indefinitely by the police.

The penalty of administrative monitoring thus affected three generations from the time the Tunisian criminal code was drafted in the 1920s. Whether in its legal, judicially mandated form, or in the de facto form practiced by the police, administrative monitoring affected thousands of Tunisians of different generations.

The totalitarianism of administrative monitoring is also apparent in the fact that it grants the executive branch of power comprehensive control over a re-leased political prisoner's everyday affairs and activities and over the details of their public and private lives.

Administrative monitoring primarily targeted former political prisoners via their social status. Prisoners whose professional positions (including primary and secondary school teachers, university professors, medical doctors, engi-neers, veterinarians, agronomists, judges, lawyers, accountants, researchers, and entrepreneurs) granted them a certain social standing based on prevalent social norms would not have been able to resume the same occupations or reclaim the same social identity after their release. They were often forced to make a living from other jobs that granted them a lower social standing within the socially defined hierarchy of occupations. Moreover, political prisoners would often spend long periods after release relying on their families for financial support, unable to find a job that would allow them to meet their basic needs. Even when the former political prisoner did find a job, there was still a chance that security agents would intervene to have them fired. Released political prisoners would thus find themselves unable to support themselves and their families and were left with their self-image and self-esteem hollowed out. Things were worse for those prisoners who left prison with chronic illness or physical disability, or, worse, malignant illnesses that threatened to shorten what little time they had left with their families. Former prisoners in these positions regularly found themselves unable to reclaim their former role in family life or fulfill the duties performed by others during their absence, which they were expected to resume after release.

# Tunisia

*Timeline*

March 20, 1956    Tunisia gained its independence from France after two years of negotiations between the French and the Neo-Destour (New Constitution) Party, thus ending the colonization of the country since 1883. Habib Bourguiba became the first prime minister.

1956    Bourguiba immediately made fundamental changes in Tunisian society regarding religion and education and led a gender-equity campaign. On August 13, 1956, the Code of Personal Status was enacted. Women had the right to consent to marriage, and a minimum age of marriage was enacted. Divorce was allowed, while polygamy was abolished. Religious courts were suppressed in favor of government courts.

1957    The monarchy was abolished, and Tunisia was proclaimed a republic.

1961    Tunisia demands that the French evacuate a former colonial naval base in Bizerte, which was crucial to France's operations in neighboring Algeria. The French responded with air strikes and a ground incursion. Some 630 Tunisians were killed. A battle ensued between Tunisian forces and French paratroopers.

1963    France pulls out of Bizerte.

1963    Perspectives, a new Left group, was established after Bourguiba dissolved the Tunisian Communist Party. Perspectives was highly critical of the Bourguiba regime on both domestic and foreign policies.

1967    At the onset of the Arab-Israeli War, Perspectives leaders drew large crowds near the British and American embassies

|      | in the capital, demonstrating against the Bourguiba regime's complicity, which it accused of collusion with the West in support of Israel. Perspectives member Mohamed Ben Jennet was sentenced to twenty years of forced labour. |
|------|------|
| 1968 | Bourguiba created a special court to punish activists, the majority of whom were from Perspectives who took part in university-wide student strikes in March 1968. The regime ultimately convicted more than eighty protesters, women among them, for crimes against the state. Torture was widely used to extract confessions. Many activists and Perspectives members had been forced underground owing to state repression. |
| 1975 | Bourguiba centralized power. Sick and aging Bourguiba was elected president for life. |
| 1981 | First multiparty parliamentary elections since independence. President Bourguiba's party wins by a landslide, a result received with cynicism and dismay by the opposition. Meanwhile, an Islamist opposition was developing around the Islamic Tendency Movement (Mouvement de la Tendance Islamique). |
| 1981 | A wave of arrests swept down on the MTI. Sentences of up to ten years of imprisonment were imposed on some sixty leaders and activists. A certain number who had fled were sentenced in absentia. |
| 1984 | Intifadat al-Khubz (Bread Uprising) over an increase in the price of bread. Bourguiba accused the MTI of being behind the protests. He sent in the army and initiated a fierce campaign against the MTI. |
| 1986 | The national elections were boycotted by the major opposition parties. |
| 1987 | More than three thousand supporters of the MTI had been detained, including many women activities. Torture was used against these detainees. |
| 1987 | Bourguiba was declared mentally unfit to rule and was removed from office by General Zine El Abidine Ben Ali, whom he had appointed as prime minister a month earlier. |
| 1989 | Ben Ali wins presidential elections. He goes on to be reelected four more times, the last time in 2009. His promises to |

promote stronger economic growth and extend human rights and multiparty democracy were not fulfilled.

| | |
|---|---|
| 2006 | Authorities launch a campaign against the Islamic headscarves worn by some women. |
| 2010 | Vegetable seller Mohamed Bouazizi sets himself on fire after police confiscate his cart. His death and funeral spark protests over unemployment, corruption, and repression. |
| January 2011 | Autocrat Zine El Abidine Ben Ali flees to Saudi Arabia, as Tunisia's revolution triggers uprisings across the Arab world. |
| 2011 | Moderate Islamist party Ennahda (MTI), banned under Bourguiba and Ben Ali, wins most seats in the election after the revolution and forms a coalition with secular parties to plan a new constitution. |
| 2014 | Beji Caid Essebsi, who served as the minister of foreign affairs (1981–86), wins Tunisia's first free presidential election. Ennahda joins the ruling coalition. |
| 2014 | Parliament approves a new constitution guaranteeing personal freedoms and rights for minorities and splitting power between the president and prime minister. |

# Contributors

**Hana Abdouli** is fifty-four, married, and a native of Sidi Bouzid governorate. She is a nurse, president of a women's organization, and member of Sidi Bouzid municipality's Committee for Women and the Family. "During the long twenty-three years of dictatorship, I wasn't promoted once. My father stood up to all forms of tyranny, injustice, and nepotism and was imprisoned in 1969 for his opposition to the behavior of local officials. After getting married, I scaled back my trade-union activism, because my husband is also a political and union activist and dissident."

**Hamida Ahmed Ajengui** is forty-eight and has four children. "I couldn't continue my education at age eighteen; I wasn't allowed, because I wore the hijab. Instead, I studied media at a private school, but I still couldn't work after getting my diploma because veiled women weren't accepted in the workplace.

"I took part in the peaceful student protests and got involved in social work with the families of detainees and people who'd had to flee their homes or been affected by the repression of 1990. It was dangerous to get involved in that sort of thing at the time, given the risks posed by police harassment and the ruling party's "vigilance committees." I was harassed and eventually arrested for the first time in September 1991 in the corridors of the state security information service in Tunis. I was held for thirteen days and subjected to various kinds of torture: I was sexually assaulted, hung in the so-called *poulet roti* (roast chicken) position for hours, and threatened with rape. I was arrested a second time in January 1992 and sentenced to six months' prison. And because I refused to give up the struggle, I was arrested a third time and sentenced to a year in prison in 1993–94.

"After my release, I waited for my fiancé to be released from prison too, and we got married in 1996. We went through many more years of persecution and administrative monitoring and struggled to make ends meet and live with dignity.

"Right after the revolution I became involved in human rights work, which is how I came to join an organization called Tunisian Women. I was on the organizing committee at the first public meeting of more than three hundred women that took place in Tunis's convention center in 2012.

"I took part in the 'Preserving Memory' project with the International Association of Prisoners and the Tunisian Justice Network, in which we sought to document the memories of prisoners through writing, poetry, images, and letters and exhibited them in Avenue de la Revolution in Tunis. I also participated in a short documentary called *Hajar al-Wad*.

"When the Truth and Dignity Commission was established, I was deeply committed to making its work a success. At Tunisian Women, we encouraged women to submit their files to the commission and to trust that their cases would be dealt with fairly. When the first public hearings took place, I gave my testimony, which shocked and affected many Tunisians and contributed to the success of the process. I am also a founding member of the Tunisian Dignity and Rehabilitation Coalition, which was established in 2017 by thirty human rights organizations to give voice to victims regardless of their political allegiances and to provide continuity after the Truth and Dignity Commission concluded its work at the end of 2018."

**Bouraouia Akkari**. "I studied in the Bourguiba era and endured harassment as a high school student. I was among those expelled in 1981 after the introduction of Circular 108. I was arrested in 1987 in my first year of university and detained for a month and a half in Tunis; my family lived in Sousse and had no idea where I was being held. We weren't interrogated during our detention, so the other detainees and I went on hunger strike until the security chief came to negotiate with us and accepted our demands. We were released without our identity papers. I continued my studies and earned a certificate in jurisprudence but was banned from working under Ben Ali's reign."

**Hasna Ben Abid** is university educated, and was born in the 1960s. "From an early age, I was deeply attached to freedom, and I shared my generation's concern for the collective good in politics, culture, and art. I wanted change. That dream came at an enormous cost, but our determination, and our dream, was greater.

"Marrying my life partner was the fulfillment of principles that we committed to when we first met. The first blow came just a few days after we got engaged, with his arrest during the bread riots. It was the start of many years of pain; our wounds had hardly healed when the next blow came. The year 1986 was a decisive one: the regime was weakened, and the young population was strong willed. Two years followed in which my partner was repeatedly kidnapped, harassed, and imprisoned, and then the same thing was repeated in the early nineties—only this time it was longer, two decades that crushed our will to live. It was a deeply distressing time when we were under siege by the enemies of freedom, and even our own relatives.

"His letters were like welcome rain during those long arid years. He wrote to me about the cold in Kasserine prison, about the cruelty of the guards and the kindness of his visitors; the darkness was far deeper and crueler, though, at El Kef prison, which was built by the colonizers to crush the nationalists' will to resist. The postindependence state had also inherited the remote country estate of a former colonizer and turned it into Grombalia prison, where it locked up activists who did not share its ideology and vision. Yet despite everything, we didn't lose hope, and here I am today, living my dream of a Tunisia bathed in freedom."

**Jomaa Ben Ali** was born in 1992 and holds a *licence appliquée* degree in English. She comes from Kebili governorate in the south of Tunisia. "I write to affirm that writing is one of the most powerful ways of conveying truth."

**Chafika Ben Hammouda** was born in El Mida, Nabeul governorate, on December 30, 1970. She was arrested by the Research and Investigation Brigade of Nabeul on November 15, 1991, and detained for twenty-one days, accused of wearing the hijab in violation of Circular 108. She died on May 17, 2021.

**Nouha Dimassi** was born on April 14, 1993, in Nabeul. Daughter of two political prisoners, she is a philosophy teacher.

**Najet Gabsi** was born on February 18, 1969, in Bir Ali Ben Khélifa, Sfax governorate. "I was arrested on December 5, 1991, as I left the law school in Sousse and was held in the civil prison there for four and a half months before being transferred to Messaadine prison for another month and a half. On June 4, 1992, I left for the great prison of society where I remained until my liberation was announced by the revolution of December 17, 2010–January 14, 2011. Maybe it's selfish of me to have used this piece of writing to make my voice heard and share personal pain, but my hope is that writing about this part of my experience will help enrich the prison literature of women; I rely on the humanity of my brothers in hoping they will accept me despite our differences."

**Katharine Halls** is an Arabic-to-English translator. Her translation, with Adam Talib, of Raja Alem's novel *The Dove's Necklace* received the 2017 Sheikh Hamad Award for Translation and International Understanding and was short-listed for the Saif Ghobash Banipal Prize. Her stage translations have been performed at the Royal Court, the Edinburgh Festival, and across Europe and the Middle East.

**Mylène Hammi** is twenty-three years old. She is a civil society activist and psychology student at the Faculté des Sciences Humaines et Sociales de Tunis. "I write out of a conviction that suffering is passed from generation to generation like a genetic inheritance and that creativity is born out of pain. I began writing at a young age and wrote about everything but politics and human rights—because before the revolution of January 14, 2011, citizens had no right to criticize or even discuss anything connected to the state. Having a relative who was a dissident in itself prompted me to ask all sorts of questions. I never had an answer to the question of why I wrote, until the revolution; it was like moving from total darkness out into the open, and that darkness I previously lived in transformed into an even greater desire to broach the subjects I couldn't talk about before. I am also interested in the psychological aspect of oppression's effects, the ramifications of taking away a person's freedoms, and the impact of punishments that can be inflicted on a person simply because they see their own psyche and that of others differently from those around them."

**Houneida Jrad** is a civil society activist and psychology student. "I wasn't directly affected by the dictatorship, but I used to see things that happened, threats, which I couldn't find a satisfactory explanation for at the time. It became clear to me that there was a certain way of dressing and certain kinds of activities that weren't allowed, though I didn't understand why. Until the revolution—then I understood everything that was previously hidden from sight."

**Virginie Ladisch** is a senior expert in truth seeking and reparative justice at the International Center for Transitional Justice. She currently leads ICTJ's work in the United States and Australia, as well as its work on mental health and psychosocial support. She has provided guidance and technical expertise to a wide range of transitional justice approaches across the globe, including in Canada, Colombia, Côte d'Ivoire, Cyprus, Liberia, the Gambia, Kenya, Nepal, Tunisia, and Uganda. Across all her work, Ladisch focuses on how engaging citizens in transitional justice processes can serve to catalyze broader public debate and ongoing civic activism. She has expertise in convening and facilitating dialogues to advance truth seeking and reparative justice, particularly with those individuals excluded from or on the margins of society, including minority groups, Indigenous peoples, women, adolescents, and youth. Committed to listening to survivors and problem solving with them, Ladisch seeks to open spaces for more inclusive participation in policy and programming discussions.

**Soulefa Mabrouk** was born in El Djem, Mahdia, on January 7, 1971. She is a graduate of Tunis's College of Visual Arts and holds an master's in heritage studies from the Université 9 Avril de Tunis. An artist, her work has been featured in a number of solo shows as well as group exhibitions of painting and photography.

**Chahla Mahjoubi** is in her fifties. She is a native of Kebili governorate in southern Tunisia. "The constant relay of events around me bewilders me, and I have only one friend and savior: my pen, whose letters and lines create forms that become new forms and take me to a supportive place of comfort and harmony."

**Brinda J. Mehta** is the Germaine Thompson Professor of French and Francophone Studies at Mills College at Northeastern University. She is the author of five books, including the award-winning *Dissident Writings of Arab Women: Voices against Violence* (2014) and *Diasporic (Dis)-locations: Indo-Caribbean Women Writers Negotiate the Kala Pani* (2004). Her numerous other publications include sixty-five articles and book chapters on postcolonial literature, several book reviews and interviews, and three coedited volumes on postcolonial Global South intellectual traditions. She is completing her sixth book, *The Wounds of War and Conflict in Women's Writings from North Africa and the Middle East.*

**Aouatef Mezghani** was born on May 6, 1966, in the Sakiet Ezzit area of Sfax. She has three sons and three grandchildren and is finance and administration manager at a group of companies. She was arrested on May 12, 1992, and spent three months in Sfax civil prison, followed by seven years under administrative monitoring.

**Sawsen Mgadla** is twenty-five years old and a native of Sfax. She is a senior pub-lic health nurse and blogger. "Perhaps my main aim in writing this piece was to draw attention to the aftereffects of repression. A regime may fall, but the fear it has provoked doesn't easily subside; it lurks inside everyone who has lived with its injustice. We must overcome that fear in order to live."

**Malika Missaoui** was born on March 14, 1966, in Menzel Bouzelfa, Nabeul gov-ernorate. She is the wife of a political prisoner and has two children. "I worked while my husband was in prison so as to support myself and give him some dig-nity by visiting him and bringing him a *quffa*. I visited him in every prison he was held in, even though many were far away—9 Avril, Harboub in Médenine, Borj Erroumi. The only exception was Rjim Maatoug in the deep south, which was impossible to get to. I used to keep bees with another wife of a prisoner, who I met outside 9 Avril prison, and in 1994 we were arrested for assisting the families of prisoners."

**Khadija Salah** was born in 1963 in Kebili governorate and is an agricultural en-gineer. She is a widow and does not have children. "I earned my degree in engi-neering in 1988, but because of my activism, my ideas, and the way I dressed, I was systematically excluded and harassed. I was banned from public- and even private-sector work, which caused problems for my family, and I only found em-ployment after the revolution. This had a major impact on all aspects of my life, and deprived me of the chance to be a mother."

**Mounira Ben Kaddour Toumi** is a mother of two and grandmother of five. Born to a Tunisian father and an Italian mother, she grew up between two cultures. She studied literature at university and speaks four languages: Arabic, French, English, and Italian. She worked in tourism for several years and also as a hotel manager. She enjoys reading, intellectual activities, classical music, and cooking. Toumi was a member of the Lions Club in the 1980s and was active in human rights after the revolution. She believes in tolerance and mutual assistance and dreams of a society characterized by peace and fraternity.

**Christalla Yakinthou** is a practice-focused political scientist at the University of Birmingham, England. She has worked in transitional justice for the past fifteen years as a practitioner, adviser, and scholar and is committed to bridging the gaps between practice and academia. Christalla focuses on supporting greater survivor and activist ownership of transitional justice processes and on building more trustful, engaged, and inclusive societies. She provides support to victim and survivor associations, NGOs, governments and intergovernmental organizations. She originally worked in constitutional design for divided societies before specializing in transitional justice. Her most recent publications include *Transitional Justice, International Assistance, and Civil Society: Missed Connections* (2018), with Paige Arthur.

**Nariman Youssef** is a Cairo-born, London-based translator and researcher. She holds a master's degree in translation studies from the University of Edinburgh and works between Arabic and English. Nariman specializes in translating for the arts and heritage sectors and currently manages a small translation team at the British Library.

**Haifa Zangana** is an Iraqi writer and human rights activist. She is the author of three novels, four short story collections, and a study, *The Braids of Iraqi Women Are Plaited with Uranium* (2014). Her English-language publications include *City of Widows: An Iraqi Woman's Account of War and Resistance, Dreaming of Baghdad, and the Torturer in the Mirror* (2007), with Ramsey Clark. She is a founding member of the International Association of Contemporary Iraqi Studies (IACIS) and Iraqi women's organization Tadhamun (Solidarity). She edited *A Party for Thaera: Palestinian Women Writing Life* (2021), a collection of writings by Palestinian women former prisoners.

She was an adviser for the United Nations Development Program report *Towards the Rise of Women in the Arab World* (2005) and consultant on the United Nations Economic and Social Commission for Western Asia's reports *Arab Integration and Towards Justice in the Arab World*, which was withdrawn by the UN general secretary.